Salvation

Salvation

EXPLORING GOD'S
ANSWER FOR YOUR
GREATEST NEED

CHARLES R. SWINDOLL

with study helps by Val Harvey

BROADMAN PRESS
NASHVILLE, TENNESSEE

This volume is affectionately
dedicated to four faithful men:

————————

Cyril Barber
Bill Butterworth
David Lien
Bill Watkins

————————

who serve behind the scenes at Insight
for Living, giving counsel and
encouragement to those who hurt,
finding in Scripture the foundation of
their faith. I am indebted to each man
for his unswerving commitment to
God's truth, his unselfish ministry to
people in need, his unceasing
discipline to stay at an endless task,
and his unsurpassed loyalty to my wife
and me as friends.

Contents

Introduction

For years I have wanted to write on doctrine . . . Bible doctrine. My flesh has been willing, but my spirit has been weak. That calls for an explanation.

The need for knowledge of the Scripture is obvious. Everywhere I turn I meet or hear about well-meaning Christians who are long on zeal but short on facts . . . lots of enthusiasm and motivation but foggy when it comes to scriptural truth.

They have a deep and genuine desire to be used by God, to reach the lost, to serve in the church, to invest their energies in "the kingdom of God and His righteousness," but their doctrinal foundation is shifting sand rather than solid rock. The result is predictable: They are at the mercy of their emotions, flying high one day and scraping the bottom the next. A frustrating yo-yo syndrome.

I know. For more years than I care to remember, I, too, climbed and tumbled, soared, and submerged, thought I knew the scoop, then later discovered how off-target I really was. The whole miserable mess leaves a person filled with doubt and disillusionment, grossly lacking in confidence, not to mention having that awful feeling of being exposed. At that point, most Christians decide to pack it in lest they get caught again in a similar position of vulnerability. You and I may be amazed to know how many have retreated into the background scenery of passivity simply because their ignorance of the basic building blocks caused them embarrassment.

Like I said, the need is obvious. Being a fixer-upper type, I am prompted to jump in with both feet and crank out a pile of pages that will provide the doctrinal ammunition so

9

many Christians need. That's why I said my flesh is willing. But since I am also a let's-be-realistic type, I am reluctant. Among the last things believers need is another dull volume on doctrine. Sterile and unapplied theology interests no one living in the real world. Most of those books wind up as great (and expensive!) doorstops. They also make a good impression when the pastor drops by for a visit and sees them lying there, freshly dusted, on the coffee table. And there is nothing like wading through thick theological works late at night to cure your battle with insomnia. Who hasn't come close to fracturing his nose on an eight-pound volume while trying to make it past page 3 in the prone position?

That's why my spirit is weak. Deep within me has been this growing fear of just pumping out another thick, boring book on doctrine that looks good but reads bad.

Theology Needs to Be Interesting

Since I am committed to accuracy, clarity, and practicality, I loathe the thought of publishing something that is anything but interesting, easily understood, creative—and yes, even captivating. See why my desire to write a book on doctrine has been on the back burner so long? It isn't easy to communicate the deepest truths of the Bible in an interesting manner. It has taken years for me to be convinced that it can be done . . . and even more years to be convinced that I may be able to do it. The chapters that follow are my best effort at accomplishing this objective. Only time will tell whether I have achieved my desire.

If my stuff makes sense, if the average individual is able to follow my thinking, picture the scenes, grasp my logic, come to similar conclusions, and later pass on a few of those thoughts to someone else, then the book will have made the impact I desired. But if it lacks real substance, or if the reader discovers it requires a graduate degree to track my thoughts, or even if it proves to be true to the biblical text yet comes across as tedious and pedantic, then my face, I can assure you, will be as red as your nose.

Introduction

The Need to Improve Theology's Reputation

Frankly, theology has gotten a bum rap. Just ask around. Make up a few questions and try them on for size in your church. You'll see. Many folks, if they are candid with you, will confess a distaste for sound biblical doctrines. Sound theology, like Rodney Dangerfield, "don't get no respect." You question that? Then let me suggest you do your own personal survey among some Christians. Ask things like:

• Ever made a study of the doctrines in the Bible?

• How would you respond if your pastor announced plans to bring a series of pulpit messages on several "important theological subjects"?

• Do you believe that all Christians ought to know where they stand doctrinally, or is that more the business of the clergy?

• When you hear the word *theology*, do you have a mental image of something interesting and stimulating? Or do you honestly think, *Dull stuff . . . please don't bore me?*

• On a scale of one to ten (ten being most important), how high would you rate a knowledge of theology?

• Can you remember a doctrinal sermon—or one lesson on theology you were involved in—that you actually *enjoyed?*

• Choosing your preference, rearrange these topics in the order you consider most interesting and timely. Which interests you the most? The least? Give each a number from one to seven.

_____ a biographical look at a biblical character

_____ a verse-by-verse analysis of a book in the New Testament

_____ a serious study of biblical doctrines

_____ what God's Word teaches about the home and family

_____ moral, social, and ethical issues according to Scripture

_____ biblical principles for success and personal motivation

———— Proverbs made practical for today

Unless you are most unusual, the study of doctrine would be ranked toward the bottom, if not altogether in last place. Compared to success principles on the home and family, "a serious study of biblical doctrines" does not seem nearly as important or relevant to most evangelical congregations. Yet, believe it or not, at the very heart of all those other topics is a great deal of theology.

It is surprising for most Christians to hear that their doctrinal position determines their interpretation and application of Scripture—whether or not they have ever declared themselves doctrinally. What roots are to a tree, the doctrines are to the Christian. From them we draw our emotional stability, our mental food for growth, as well as our spiritual energy and perspective on life itself. By returning to our roots, we determine precisely where we stand. We equip ourselves for living the life God designed for us to live.

Why Is Doctrine Often So Dull?

If all this is true, then why does the mere mention of theology turn off so many people? Why are most churches full of people programmed to think that doctrine is a synonym for dullness and boredom?

At the risk of appearing ultracritical, I'll be frank with you. Much of the problem lies with theologians who have done a poor job of communicating their subject. No offense, theological scholars, but you are notorious for talking only to yourselves. The language you employ is clergy code-talk, woefully lacking in relevance and reality. The terms you use are in-house jargon, seldom broken down into manageable units for people who aren't clued in. You may be accurate and certainly sincere, but your world is like the television series of yesteryear, "One Step Beyond." Please understand that we love you and respect you. No one would dare to question your brilliance. We need your gifts in the body and we admire your ability to stay at the disciplines of your studies. We just don't understand you.

As a result, much of what you write is kept within those

cloistered chambers that intimidate people who haven't had the privilege of probing the heavenlies as you have. The majority feel a distance from you when you share your secrets. I realize that many of you wish this weren't so, but I suppose it comes with the territory.

In this book and the others in this study series, my hope is to build a bridge of theological understanding with the common man, the uninitiated individual, the person who has never been to seminary—and doesn't care to to go—but really does want to develop a solid network of doctrinal roots.

I'm interested in reaching the truck driver, the athlete, the waitress, the high school student, the person in the military service, the homemaker who has a houseful of kids at her feet, the business person whose world is practical, earthy, tough, and relentless . . . and a hundred other "types" who have the brains to absorb biblical truth but lack the time and patience to look up every sixth or seventh word in a dictionary.

I therefore make no apology for approaching various subjects in a different way than standard theologians. I want everyone who picks up this book to understand every word and grasp every principle, even if you don't agree with them. (To disagree with me is your privilege—I expect it. In fact, I invite it. But to misunderstand or to *fail* to understand what I'm getting at would be tragic.)

I freely confess that I want you to enjoy this journey . . . to find out that discovering doctrine and seeing its importance can encourage you like nothing else. I want us to laugh together, as well as think together, as we dig into *the Book*. It's been my observation for the past twenty-five years of ministry that there is no subject too deep for anyone to understand if the material is presented creatively and clearly, sparked periodically by humor, and accompanied by illustrations that let plenty of life in. All this is true of folks who really want to learn.

By the way, that brings up another reason doctrine is dull to some people. As I implied earlier, they have a built-in, long-standing *prejudice* against it. Somehow, they have convinced themselves that (a) they don't need to fuss around with heady stuff like that since they aren't doing "full-time ministry," or (b) even if they made a study of the doctrines, all that knowledge would be of little practical value. In subtle ways these two excuses tend to plug their ears and clog the learning process.

Without trying to perform an overkill, both of those excuses are totally erroneous. Because every Christian is "doing full-time ministry," being theologically informed and equipped could not be more important. And since when does a knowledge of important facts lack practical value? If I recall Jesus' words correctly, that which makes us free is knowing the truth. It's ignorance that binds us, not knowledge. Furthermore, we are left defenseless before the cults and other persuasive false teachers if we lack this solid network of doctrinal roots. As I stated earlier, it stabilizes us.

An Approach that Will Keep Things Interesting

Before we get underway, let me explain my plan of approach.

I have no intention of writing an exhaustive theological treatment on all the biblical doctrines. (If you happen to be a perfectionist, expecting every jot and tittle to be addressed in this volume or the others in this series, please read that sentence again.) My plan is to offer a broad-brush approach to most of the essential points of evangelical truth. If you find certain details are not covered to your satisfaction or if you observe that some subjects of interest to you are not even mentioned, just remember that is on purpose. I'm hoping to whet your appetite for a much more intense and thorough study *on your own* once you've begun to get excited about these essential areas. Who knows? Maybe one day *you'll* be the one who will write a more thorough and analytical work. Be my guest.

You'll also want to keep a Bible handy. I'll try to quote as many of the main verses and passages as possible. But there will be times that I will give an additional reference or two which you might want to look up right then. If you have the time, please do that. Before too long you will begin to feel much more at home in the Scriptures. And use a good study Bible rather than a loose paraphrase or a copy of just the New Testament.

There are a number of study tools that make the Bible and its people come to life for you. *Commentaries* explore books of the Bible and tell you what scholars have discovered about the writers of the books, the times in which they lived, and what the Scriptures mean. *Bible encyclopedias, dictionaries,* and *handbooks* contain information about the people, places, and events in the Bible. They often include drawings and pictures to help you put yourself in the first-century world. *Bible atlases* have maps that show how the Holy Land looked at various times throughout history. Atlases usually give background information about governments and geography. *Concordances* tell you where words appear in the Bible. Pick a word like *love*; look it up just like you would in a dictionary; and you'll find a list of verses in which *love* is used. If you're serious about Bible study, you'll want to stop by a bookstore and invest in a good Bible handbook, atlas, and concordance. You'll be surprised how much those resources will add to your study.

At the end of the first chapter of each part of this book you will note several thoughts I call "Root Issues." These are simply practical suggestions designed to help you keep the doctrines out of the realm of sterile theory and in touch with the real world. To get the most out of these, I'd recommend that you purchase a handy-sized spiral notebook—your personal "Root Issues Notebook"—to record your thoughts, observations, and responses. Each chapter concludes with study questions. "Extending Your Roots" helps you explore what we've been talking about. "Taproot" takes you even further in your study of each doctrine. Don't be afraid to write your answers in this book. It's yours—make it personal.

Growing Deep in the Christian Life: Salvation

Ten Major Areas of Doctrine

Finally, the outline I want to follow will be interwoven in this series of five study guides. All the doctrines I want to cover will fall within these ten major categories:

- The Bible
- God the Father
- The Lord Jesus Christ
- The Holy Spirit
- The Depravity of Humanity
- Salvation
- The Return of Christ
- Resurrection
- The Body of Christ
- The Family of God

As I mentioned earlier, the list is purposely not exhaustive, but there is plenty here to get our roots firmly in place. In fact, the better-known historic creeds down through the ages have included these ten areas. While considering this recently, I decided to write my own doctrinal credo, a statement of my personal faith. What it may lack in theological sophistication I have tried to make up for in practical terminology.

As I return to the roots of my faith, I am encouraged to find the time-honored foundations firmly intact:

- I affirm my confidence in God's inerrant Word. I treasure its truths and I respect its reproofs.
- I acknowledge the Creator-God as my Heavenly Father, infinitely perfect, and intimately acquainted with all my ways.
- I claim Jesus Christ as my Lord—very God who came in human flesh—the object of my worship and the subject of my praise.
- I recognize the Holy Spirit as the third member of the Godhead, incessantly at work convicting, convincing, and comforting.
- I confess that Adam's fall into sin left humanity without the hope of heaven apart from a new birth, made possible by the Savior's death and bodily resurrection.
- I believe the offer of salvation is God's love-gift to all. Those who accept it by faith, apart from works, become new creatures in Christ.

- I anticipate my Lord's promised return, which could occur at any moment.
- I am convinced that all who have died will be brought
  back from beyond—believers to everlasting communion
  with God and unbelievers to everlasting separation from
  God.
- I know the Lord is continuing to enlarge His family, the
  universal body of Christ, over which He rules as Head.
- I am grateful to be a part of a local church which exists to
  proclaim God's truth, to administer the ordinances, to
  stimulate growth toward maturity, and to bring glory to
  God.

With confidence and joy, I declare this to be a statement
of the essentials of my faith.

That's where I stand . . . sort of a preview of coming attrac-
tions. Now it's time for you to dig in and discover where you
stand. With God's help I think you will find this study one of
the most important and interesting projects you have ever
undertaken. You may even get so "fanatical" about your
faith that your whole perspective on life changes.

Come to think of it, that's exactly what Christianity is
supposed to do . . . change our lives.

I wish to thank my long-term, splendid secretary as I have
so many times before. Helen Peters has done it again. Without regard for her own needs and preferences, she has deci-
phered my hand scratching, typed and retyped my manu-
script, verified my footnotes, corrected my spelling, and
helped me meet my deadlines. "Thank you" seems hardly
sufficient to declare the depth of my gratitude. I also want
to thank Val Harvey for her excellent work in writing the
study questions for each of the volumes in this series.

And now let's dig in. You have stumbled your way
through shifting sand long enough. May these books on
Bible doctrine give you just the help you need so that you
can stand firmly and finally on a foundation that is solid as
rock.

Charles R. Swindoll
Fullerton, California

Part

I

Sin

1 From Creation to Corruption

Philosophers can be terribly confusing. What they call deep and profound we're tempted to consider dull and vague. One honest soul put it rather well: "Philosophers are people who talk about things they don't understand . . . but they make it sound like it's your fault."

Well, not always. Sometimes they are right on target. There are times philosopher types put it so succinctly that you can't improve upon it. For example there's that age-old axiom:

> Wherever there is a thing, there must have been a preceding thought . . . and where there is a thought, there must have been a thinker.

Take the place where you sit right now . . . just look around. It reflects thought. Someone had in mind that someday in the future somebody would be sitting there. Therefore, a design was planned that would make it possible for you to sit where you're sitting and for you to enjoy the surroundings in which you find yourself. The place that you enjoy (the "thing") is the seat and the room you're sitting in. And as you look around, it's obvious the design was well-planned (the "thought") by someone (the "thinker") who wanted you to be comfortable. Neither the room nor the seat "just happened."

Or let's take a walk outside. I want us to look at some cars together. If possible, let's find a new one. While you're standing there admiring the beauty of that sparkling new automobile, let's imagine my saying to you rather quietly,

"You know, there are folks who believe this car is a result of someone's design . . . but I know differently. Let me tell you what really happened":

Many, many centuries ago, all this iron, glass, rubber, plastic, fabric, leather, and wires came up out of the ground. Furthermore, each substance fashioned itself into various shapes and sizes . . . and holes evolved at just the right places, and the upholstery began to weave itself together. After a while threads appeared on bolts and nuts and—amazing as it may seem—each bolt found nuts with matching threads. And gradually everything sort of screwed up tightly in place. A little later correctly shaped glass glued itself in the right places. And you see these tires? They became round over the years. And they found themselves the right size metal wheels. And they sort of popped on. They also filled themselves with air somehow. And the thing began to roll down the street.

And one day, many, many years ago—centuries, really— some people were walking along and they found this vehicle sitting under a tree. And one of them looked at it and thought, "How amazing. I think we should call it 'automobile.'" But there's more! These little automobiles have an amazing way of multiplying themselves year after year . . . even changing ever so slightly to meet the demands of the public. Actually, that process is called "automutations."

I have a sneaking suspicion that, having heard all that, you would want to remove yourself from my presence. You probably would call my wife and ask if I've been feeling well lately.

Let's get serious! I would be a first-class lunatic if I believed that automobiles evolved. The auto is in the category of a thing, and it reflects thought. And for there to have been thought given to the design of the automobile, there must have been a thinker—a designer.

Now, multiply that design process an infinite number of times, and you find yourself in touch with the universe, which God said He made. In fact, He was bold enough to say in the first sentence of the Bible that He *created* the heavens and the earth. Only ten words appear in the opening sentence of our Bible (actually only seven words in the Hebrew Bible), and yet that sentence has become a watershed of controversy. Why? Because people far more brilliant than we have come up with the theory that the world really wasn't created; it has evolved, as has mankind—and then they're off into the meanderings of scientific imaginations expressed in sophisticated gobbledygook.

To complicate things, many people believe the theories so firmly that when they read Genesis 1:1, they respond with words like, "The verse may be characterized as a veritable treasure house of myths" and "The statement is a joke, an absolute impossibility."

Why? Why would people with bright minds, why would competent and intelligent men and women embrace the theories of man rather than the statement of God when it comes to the creation of a world and the origin of humankind? After all, they are people of research and scholarship and facts. They'll tell you they don't believe in blind chance. But when they come to our universe and the people who fill it, it's just too much. They cannot bring themselves to believe in divine creation. Why?

Perhaps it's just too simple for the sophisticated. Obviously, it requires a belief in a thinker, a supreme being greater than they. And, to them, that's a leap in the dark, a thought too risky to embrace. But it's at that very point that I find those who deny creation so illogical. *They* are the ones guilty of making a leap in the dark when they embrace the theories of evolution. The existence of our world and mankind defies all mathematical calculations of chance!

This was driven home to me many years ago when I came across an illustration from a noted scientist. As I recall, he was a former president of the New York Academy of Sciences. It went something like this: "Let's say I have ten pennies and I mark each one with a number (one to ten), then place all ten in your pocket. I would ask you to give your pocket a good shake so that the pennies are no longer in any order in your pocket. What chance would I have to reach in and pull out penny number one? One in ten. Let's say I put the penny back, then I reach again into your pocket and draw out penny number two. My chance of doing that would be one in a hundred. Putting the penny back, if I were to reach in and draw out penny number three, my chances would jump to one in a thousand. If I were able to continue doing the same, in successive order, right up through number nine, do you know what my chance would be by the time I got to the number ten and pulled it out of your pocket? *One in ten billion.* If I pulled that off you would say, 'The game is fixed!' My answer: 'You're right—and so is creation.' "

How different from the theories of man! Read this "explanation" very carefully. Try not to smile.

By and large, cosmologists have become accustomed to the idea that the Universe began with an initial singularity of infinite density and infinitesimally small volume. This idea is strongly supported by the singularity theorems which Penrose and Hawking produced in the 1960s. But now, in an about-face that has come from a consideration of quantum mechanical effects on the origin of the Universe, Hawking and colleagues suggest that the Universe had a non-singular beginning followed by a period of very rapid expansion (which goes under the name of inflation) and then a transition to the conventional development described by the hot big-bang model. A longstanding problem of cosmology, to explain the origin of the density fluctuations that are needed to account for the galaxies, is solved along the way by quantum fluctuations.[1]

I am not trying to be cute or clever. That is an actual quotation from a highly respected scholar who has bought into a humanistic answer to how the universe began.

In the chapters that follow, we'll be looking at how humans came to be and how they came to sin. We'll explore what it means to be human and what sin does to our lives. Then we'll find out that there is a remedy, a way to restore what sin has broken.

Root Issues

1. Have you thought of work—your daily tasks—as a curse? A dread? Applying what you've learned about the power of God's Holy Spirit within you, ask the Lord to give you a new vision—a new attitude toward the "garden" He has given you to tend. If difficult on-the-job relationships with other people have contributed to your work anxieties, ask a friend to join you in praying specifically for the individuals and situations that produce the most tension. Don't depend on your own strength!

2. Children have no difficulty at all accepting the truths of biblical creation. It's *adults* who are bothered by all the phony intellectual baggage that accompanies this vital subject. Take the first opportunity you find to talk to a young child about the wonder of God's creation as revealed in Genesis. If possible, highlight the discussion by a walk outside to observe things such as flowers, leaves, trees, and so on. Take time to carefully note the child's observations and questions. The questions can be tough—like, why did God make flies? But you'll never have a better opportunity to gain a fresh, unspoiled perspective on God's marvelous handiwork. Pray with the child to thank God for all that He has made.

3. In the days of their innocence, Adam and Eve seemed to have a special time of day set aside to walk and talk with their God. When they didn't show up one day both they and God knew something was terribly wrong. Do you have a daily appointment with God—a special time reserved for just the two of you . . . a time when you give yourself to reading His Word and listening for His footsteps . . . for His voice? You've probably heard preachers and teachers suggest a *regular, daily* time with the Lord again and again. What will it take for you to begin? Ask someone to "hold you accountable" to spend time alone with the Lord each day— even if for only five or ten minutes. Ask your friend to check

on you once a week for three or four weeks. If you have no idea how to start a consistent time with God, ask a Christian friend or check at a Christian book store for the little booklet *Seven Minutes with God.*

4. A problem we all have at one time or another is allowing unconfessed sin to build up in our lives—cutting us off from fellowship with our Lord and generally making us miserable. What specific things happened in David's life when he refused to confess his sin?(Ps. 32:3-4). What happens in your life when you have held onto certain sins, resisting the Holy Spirit's voice? What did David find to rejoice about after he "came clean" before the Lord? Think of at least one practical way you might remind yourself to "keep short accounts with God"—that is, coming to Him in confession *immediately* after you become aware of sin in your life.

5. If you have not done so already, memorize what has become one of the most frequently quoted and beloved promises in all of the Bible, 1 John 1:9.

6. Identify the "danger areas" in your life—those tendencies or weaknesses that carry the greatest hazard of plunging you into sin. Carefully evaluate what activities, situations, or associations during the course of an average week bring you closest to those areas of "thin ice." (In David's case, a particular *place* on his rooftop at a particular *time* in the evening gave him a particular *view* that led him into disaster. The *situation* of idle time also seemed to be a dangerous one for the king.) Identifying these dangers is a very important step. Many need to avoid proximity to alcoholic beverages and the availability of habit-forming drugs. For others of us it's airport newsstands. Or certain situations with coworkers of the opposite sex. Or the strong urge to overeat. It is also very important to get prayer support from your spouse or a close friend. Having someone "check up on you" from time to time in these highly sensitive, highly dangerous areas can literally mean the difference between victory and defeat. We need each other! Let's call for help.

Extending Your Roots

The Bible says, "The fool says in his heart, 'There is no God' " (Ps. 53:1, NIV). The Old Testament never tries to prove that God exists. It begins by assuming that He exists and that He is the Creator of all else that exists.

Three basic questions surface when a person considers the subject of creation:

(1) Who created the universe?
(2) When was it created?
(3) How was it created?

1. Using your own creative expression (art, poetry, a letter to God or a friend), describe God as if all you knew of Him was the creation account of Genesis 1.

2. Now read the biblical account of creation from Genesis 1:1 to 2:4.

Taproot

1. God's creative work was not final in the Genesis creation. He promised the prophet Isaiah something more. Read Isaiah 65:17-25 and 66:22.

2. The apostle John saw a new creation and recorded his vision in Revelation 21. Read the chapter and answer the following questions:

(1) When the new creation occurs, what will happen to the old one?

(2) Why do you think there will no longer be a sea? (Perhaps a commentary will offer some suggestions.)

(3) In verse 5, God describes Himself as being the alpha and omega, the first and last letters of the Greek alphabet? Why do you think God chose this particular example?

(4) How did God finish the Genesis creation? Read Genesis 2:1-3.

How did Jesus conclude the work of redemption? Read John 19:30.

How did God finish the new creation? Read Revelation 21:6.

(5) How big is your God? Is the God of creation big enough to meet the needs of your life? Explain.

2 A Fresh Look at Our Roots

My interest is not in defending creation. My interest is in simply declaring the creation of humankind. Reading what Scripture records about those earliest hours of time—returning to that epochal moment when God, having made all the other things in their kind, made humankind—I find answers that make good sense.

If you have a Bible handy, open it to Genesis 1. You will see the same words repeated again and again. First, take a look at the passage:

> Then God said, "Let the earth sprout vegetation, plants yielding seed, and fruit trees bearing fruit after their kind, with seed in them, on the earth"; and it was so. And the earth brought forth vegetation, plants yielding seed after their kind, and trees bearing fruit, with seed in them, after their kind; and God saw that it was good. And there was evening and there was morning, a third day.
>
> Then God said, "Let there be lights in the expanse of the heavens to separate the day from the night, and let them be for signs, and for seasons, and for days and years; and let them be for lights in the expanse of the heavens to give light on the earth"; and it was so. And God made the two great lights, the greater light to govern the day, and the lesser light to govern the night; He made the stars also. And God placed them in the expanse of the heavens to give light on the earth, and to govern the day and the night, and to separate the light from the darkness; and God saw that it was good. And there was evening and there was morning, a fourth day.
>
> Then God said, "Let the waters teem with swarms of living

creatures, and let birds fly above the earth in the open expanse of the heavens." And God created the great sea monsters, and every living creature that moves, with which the waters swarmed after their kind, and every winged bird after its kind; and God saw that it was good. And God blessed them, saying, "Be fruitful and multiply, and fill the waters in the seas, and let birds multiply on the earth." And there was evening and there was morning, a fifth day.

Then God said, "Let the earth bring forth living creatures after their kind: cattle and creeping things and beasts of the earth after their kind"; and it was so. And God made the beasts of the earth after their kind, and the cattle after their kind, and everything that creeps on the ground after its kind; and God saw that it was good (vv. 11-25).

Did you notice the oft-repeated words "after their kind . . ." (vv. 12, 21, 24); and even three times in one verse, "after their kind, . . . after its kind"? (v. 25). Meaning what? When God created living things He maintained precise distinctions. Distinct species. These vast categories of created things and beings are spelled out in quick order in Genesis 1. And each one has a uniqueness about it, each is according to its "kind." The fowls of the air . . . the fish of the sea . . . the beasts of the field. Each one was created according to its "kind."

There is a most significant statement made in 1 Corinthians 15 which underscores the same idea:

> All flesh is not the same flesh, but there is one flesh of men, and another flesh of beasts, and another flesh of birds, and another of fish (v. 39).

God made each with a different physical texture, a different internal makeup. You can't ignore those distinctions and lump them all together and maintain the correct biblical position on creation.

Now verse 45:

> So also it is written, "The first man, Adam, became a living soul." The last Adam became a life-giving spirit.

How terribly important! Look again at those words, "The

first man." This is a translation of the Greek terms *Ho Pro-tos Anthropos.* A paraphrase might read, "the first in the category of mankind" was Adam, the first created human being. Adam's "kind" was a first. Nothing before him fell into the category of his species. In Adam we find a fully developed adult human being, equipped with intelligence and godlike capabilities from the very beginning: intelligence, emotions, will. No other living thing or living being was like *Anthropos.* No animal or fowl or fish or plant could know God or love and respond to God or obey God . . . or utilize the earth's resources in ways consistent with God's creative purposes. In other words, *Ho Protos Anthropos* was (and still is) altogether unique.

Look at Genesis 1:26.

> Then God said, "Let Us make man in Our image, according to Our likeness; and let them rule over the fish of the sea and over the birds of the sky and over the cattle and over all the earth, and over every creeping thing that creeps on the earth."

I find it very interesting, as I reflect on the philosophical axiom I quoted earlier, that the statement works in reverse order here in the creation account. First is the thinker—"And God said," Then comes the thought:

> Then God said, "Let Us make man in Our image, according to Our likeness. ''

And the *thing?* Verse 27 tells us. "God created man."

When it came to the first in the category of mankind, the pattern God followed was "in Our image." In other words, "The man will be unlike anything I have created. No other created being has a mind to know Me. No other created being has a heart to love Me. No other created being has a will to obey Me. Therefore, no other creation has an eternal destiny like this created being has. We'll make him distinct. Only humans will have *imago Dei,* the image of God, stamped on them." What a privileged position!

Extending Your Roots

1. Read or sing "How Great Thou Art." Perhaps you have a recording of the song. Meditate on the words of the song.

2. Read Job 38:4-33 and Psalm 8:1-9. Now combine the two Scripture passages into a dramatic dialogue or a responsive reading. For an example refer to the responsive readings in the back of a hymnal. Ask a friend to read about creation with you.

Taproot

1. Give at least three ways in which humans can be seen as having been made in the image of God.

2. The New Testament suggests that we are transformed into the image of Christ. What does this mean? (See Rom. 8:29; 2 Cor. 3:18; Col. 3:9-10; 1 John 3:2.)

3 | How It All Started . . . Historically

Let me reiterate a couple of observations about our creation that remain true to the present moment. *First*, I observe that humans are *unique*. We are unique because this species is the only species created in God's image, after God's likeness. *Second*, I notice that the "mankind species" is *superior*. No other creature was told to rule over anything. Verse 26, however, states, "Let [mankind] rule." The Hebrew verb is vivid: "to trample down, to dominate, to master, to prevail over." Strong words. This creature (and none other) is destined by God to dominate the world in which he finds himself. It isn't wrong to explore our world or to travel into space; it's wrong *not* to. Even though we may lose some lives in the risk of our research, we are to press forward. We are to probe into our universe. It isn't wrong to use (though not abuse) the resources of this world; it's wrong *not* to. God gave us the command to do so. It isn't wrong to take charge of the creatures that live on this world—not to abuse them, but to control them. God gave *Anthropos* that superior position.

Creation and Instruction

Listen to verse 28:

And God blessed them; and God said to them, "Be fruitful and multiply, and fill the earth, and subdue it; and rule over the fish of the sea and over the birds of the sky, and over every living thing that moves on the earth."

Now here is humankind, receiving instruction—they are

told to reproduce, and they are told to rule. In fact, they are also told to work . . . to keep the garden beautiful.

> Then the Lord God took the man and put him into the garden of Eden to cultivate it and keep it (2:15).

Work isn't a curse. We need to remember that work was created in a context of absolute innocence.

"But I thought work was a curse," you answer. No, it is the anxiety of dealing with people that's the curse. The sweat that comes to our brows because of the wrongdoing of others and our own selves, *that's* the curse. But work was originally established in a context of innocence. The earliest occupation was landscaping—the work of horticulture. It was to maintain and cultivate the garden.

And man was given one negative command, only one. It had to do with the tree in the garden called "the tree of the knowledge of good and evil." That tree is mentioned in verse 17:

> But from the tree of the knowledge of good and evil you shall not eat, for in the day that you eat from it you shall surely die.

Interesting how those last four words appear in the Hebrew: "Dying, you will die." Dying spiritually (the moment you eat from the tree), you will begin to die physically. Would Adam and Eve have lived forever had they not taken of the tree? Yes, indeed. And because they took of the tree of knowledge of good and evil, they introduced death to this world of ours—not only death but also all that precedes it by way of sickness and disease. The issue of this tree was extremely significant . . . representing a nonnegotiable command . . . plain, clear, and simple: "Don't eat of the tree of the knowledge of good and evil." There was no way Adam could have misunderstood.

Temptation and Corruption

The original story of innocence and beauty becomes a study in selfishness and tragedy beyond the warning. Genesis 3 is familiar to all Bible students—especially as it relates to the temptation in the garden, which culminates at verse 6.

> When the woman saw that the tree was good for food, and that it was a delight to the eyes, and that the tree was desirable to make one wise, she took from its fruit and ate; and she gave also to her husband with her, and he ate.

Notice the words, "she took from its fruit and ate ... and ... her husband with her and he ate." That's where all our troubles began. And the root word for all our troubles? *Depravity.*

Up until then nothing but innocence was flowing through the bloodstream of mankind. There was an enviable, uninterrupted communion with the living God, the Creator. There was the blessing and delight of walks with God, the joy of His presence, the unguarded relationship, the familiar friendship. There was an absence of rebellion, selfishness, defensiveness, and embarrassment. There was— but no longer!

At that awful moment the original couple yielded to temptation, depravity entered and contaminated the human bloodstream. Depravity intercepted innocence and ruined it, leaving mankind alienated from God. Instead of the mind being clear and full of the knowledge of God, it became clouded. And instead of possessing that once-strong love for God, humanity became resentful of God, an emotional wreck ... fragile and weak. And the will, once obedient, became rebellious.

The disease continues! Instead of adoring God, we fight with Him. Instead of believing what He says, we reject His truth. Instead of wanting to do what He would have us do, we delight in doing what *we* want to do. And to make matters even worse, instead of facing it, we cover it up. It all goes back to the original scene.

Let me show you. Verse 7 begins with the word "Then." When? Immediately after they had eaten from the forbidden tree.

Then the eyes of both of them were opened, and they knew
that they were naked . . .

Up until then they did not even know they were naked!
Adam and Eve did not realize that they were in each other's
presence without clothing. They lived in perfect and unpre-
tentious innocence. They enjoyed the delights and intima-
cies of marriage. They enjoyed an innocent nakedness in the
presence of one another—not only physically but also emotionally. They were totally comfortable, totally at ease, totally secure. But no longer!

Immediately after eating from the fruit they became (get
this) self-conscious for the first time. They knew they were
naked. And realizing their nakedness, they did the most
natural, human thing one can do—they covered up. Verse 7
continues:

they sewed fig leaves together and made themselves loin
coverings.

But their hiding isn't over, it's just begun.

And they heard the sound of the Lord God walking in the
garden in the cool of the day, and the man and his wife hid
themselves from the presence of the Lord God among the
trees of the garden (v. 8).

I'm fascinated by that word picture. As at other times, the
Creator-God is coming down the trail to meet with His creation. But how things have changed! He doesn't find man
and woman. Why? Because—

the man and his wife hid themselves from the presence of the
Lord God among the trees of the garden (v. 8*b*).

As a result of becoming self-conscious, there was an im-
mediate cover-up, personally. And then there was a hiding
from the Creator, relationally. It still goes on today. The
scene is different, but the principles are the same.

Then the Lord God called to the man, and said to him,
"Where are you?" (v. 9).

I don't know why, but people have the strange idea that

God really didn't know where Adam and Eve were. Sort of like He was stumbling around in a quandary, calling "A-a-a-a-d-a-a-am! Where a-a-a-re you, Eve? Come on, tell Me!"

No! He knew exactly where they were. He is God! His question implies, "Why are you where you are? What are you doing there? You've never hidden from Me." Embarrassed, Adam reluctantly responds:

> "I heard the sound of Thee in the garden, and I was afraid because I was naked; so I hid myself" (v. 10).

Two brand-new statements appear in Adam's confession: "I was afraid . . . I was naked." God answers, "Who told you that you were naked?"

That question seems so strange to us today, because we've never entertained such innocence. Let me ask you rather bluntly, are you aware when you're naked? I hope to shout. We know about every button that's missing, every hole in our pants or shirt, every zipper that won't stay zipped. Every time we're in public we can't think of anything else but the ripped pants or the hole in the shirt or the broken zipper. Why? Because we are self-conscious creatures. Why, the slightest hint of nakedness brings shame and embarrassment.

My wife and I were invited to minister together in Colorado Springs not long ago. Busily engaged in getting our seat selection and baggage tags at the airport in Los Angeles, we were both bending, lifting, stooping, and maneuvering our way through the process. On my final stoop-and-lift movement, I felt the seat of my trousers r-r-r-rip. Not just a tiny rip, either.

Well! All my other clothing for the trip was now sliding out of sight on the conveyer belt, heading toward our plane. I didn't have time to return home to change. I was on my own. I did all the things you have to do to keep a secret like that. I kept jerking my coattail down in the back . . . or backing up and standing near a wall. I even carried my briefcase behind me when I got on and off the plane. You're gonna laugh, but when we got to our destination, there were three flights of stairs we had to walk up to get to our room, and they were busy with people in front of us and behind us. Never before have I walked up stairs sideways, but I managed. By then, of course, the r-r-rip was really a r-r-r-r-rip!

I have Adam to thank for my embarrassment. It's all part of the depravity package. Like Adam, "I was afraid because I was naked; so I hid myself." But, unlike Adam, I wasn't found out.

God's question was pointed: "Who told you were naked?" And before Adam could answer:

> Have you eaten from the tree of which I commanded you not to eat? (v. 11).

Trouble, serious trouble, has entered the home of Adam and Eve. And it would never leave. Created in pristine innocence and flawless beauty, they now find themselves distant from the One who made them. Because at this moment depravity, the presence of sin, has invaded and polluted their lives.

God confronts them, which results in one of those unforgettable dialogues in Scripture. God speaks first with Adam, then Eve, and finally the serpent. He says to Adam: "Did you eat from the tree?"

> And the man said, "The woman whom Thou gavest to be with me, she gave me from the tree, and I ate" (v. 12).

Notice how he proceeded the confession with an alibi, a veiled statement of blame. That's also very common. Rather than, "Yes, guilty as charged," Adam says, "Now God, if it hadn't been for the woman *You* gave me, I probably would still be pure. But because of what *You* did and *she* did, well, I ate." God doesn't argue. He faces Eve next, who must have been shaking in her apron:

> And the woman said, "The serpent deceived me, and I ate" (v. 13*b*).

We will do anything on earth to keep from saying, "I am responsible, no one else." Fact is, we *love* substitutes.

That came to my mind when I found an interesting ad in a newspaper. Can't even remember which newspaper. It was called "Rent-A-Jogger," offering something like "Rent me for $1.95 and I will jog for you at least one mile each day (weather permitting) for the next year." A customer gets a suitably framed certificate, attesting to the world that "Your jogger is securing for you the benefits of a healthful glow, extraordinary stamina, an exciting muscle tone, and power-filled sense of total well-being."

"Rent-A-Jogger" was the idea of some forty-five-year-old stockbroker who is also the guy who runs for the customer. Believe it or not, within several days after the ads appeared, 322 people had sent him $1.95, which more than paid for the ads!

When it comes to wrong, we'd like to "rent a sinner." We'll do anything to keep from saying, "I have sinned." We'll cover up. We'll hide. We'll rationalize. We'll point to somebody else. We'll find a scapegoat and blame him or her. We'll do anything but say, "I have sinned."

They finally said it. And the curse that fell way back then has left us in a desperate state of affairs. Yes, the right word is *desperate*. The desperation has grown into full-blown depravity.

Extending Your Roots

God does not tell how evil came into the world. This fact has been accepted since creation. A garden was prepared with everything pleasing to life. Suddenly there comes an intrusion of the serpent and then sin. Read Genesis 3 and write in your answers or thoughts in the following spaces.

1. Describe the serpent.

What tactics did he use on the woman?

Growing Deep in the Christian Life: Salvation

The woman responded to the serpent by correcting him. Read carefully verses 2 and 3.

How had Eve changed or added to God's instruction? (Gen. 2:16-17).

What part does curiosity, desire, and attractiveness play in temptation?

2. What promise did the tempter give the woman if she would eat the fruit?

What part does lying play in temptation?

3. Why do you think Adam listened to Eve?

List some ways other people pressure you to yield to temptation.

4. Read verses 9-13. Write what God asked Adam and Eve. Then record what they said.
Question (v. 9):

Response (v. 10):
Question (v. 11):
Response (v. 12):
Question (v. 13):
Response (v. 13):
   In what ways do you sometimes try to justify yielding to temptation?

5. Based on the experience of Adam and Eve and your own observations of human nature, give a definition of sin.

 *Taproot*

   1. Jesus had just concluded a mountaintop experience. Following His baptism, the Holy Spirit led Him into the wilderness. During this time, the tempter came to Jesus. Compare the temptation experience by Jesus in the wilderness (Matt. 4:1-11; Luke 4:1-13) to the temptation of Adam and Eve. List the differences or similarities.

2. Complete the following statements:
MY TEMPTATIONS ARE:

I CAN RESIST THESE TEMPTATIONS BY:

4 Where It All Led . . . Theologically

Webster says *depraved* means, "marked by corruption or evil, perverted, crooked." It's important that you understand this is an internal disease; you can't detect it from the outside. Most folks don't "look" depraved. Most of us do a masterful job of covering up. But never doubt that underneath, deep down inside, there is this disease that eats away at us and pollutes our thoughts and our words (intellect), our relationships (emotions), and our actions (will).

One theologian describes depravity this way:

> This doctrine has suffered from many misconceptions, for the average person would define total depravity by saying that it means that man is as bad as he can be. However, if we adopt that as an acceptable definition, immediately our theology is brought into question because we know men who are not as bad as they can be. We know many men who are good men, kind men, generous men, moral men, men who contribute much in the home and in the community. Rather, the doctrine of depravity says that man is as bad *off* as he can be. There is a vast difference between being as *bad* as he can be and being as bad *off* as he can be.
>
> The doctrine of depravity has to do, not with man's estimation of man, but rather with God's estimation of man. We are the heirs of generations of the teaching of evolution which sees man in an ever-ascending spiral, rising higher and higher from the depth from which he has sprung, until finally he will reach the stars. So widely accepted is that concept that we have come somehow to feel that there is so much good in the worst of us that man is not so bad off after all. When we measure men by man, we can always find someone who is

lower than we are on the moral or ethical scale, and the comparison gives us a feeling of self-satisfaction. But the Scriptures do not measure men by man; they measure men by God who has created them. The creature is measured by the Creator and is found to be wanting.[1]

Someone said it best when he suggested, "If depravity were blue, we'd be blue all over." Cut us anywhere and we'll bleed blue. Cut into our minds and you'll find blue thoughts. Cut into our vision and there are blue images full of greed and lust. Cut into our hearts and there are blue emotions of hatred, revenge, and blame. Cut into our wills and you'll find deep blue decisions and responses.

The tragedy is we don't *look* blue! We look good, almost white at times. We look clean. We're among "the beautiful people" of the twentieth century. I think we look physically better than our world has ever looked. But there's something deep within that is depraved. It's called our nature. That's why we *can't* clean up our act. That's why we can't handle our own lust. That's why we can't say no to certain temptations. That's why we fight with each other and fight with God—realizing that we shouldn't. And yet we can't seem to stop. We can't seem to keep our promises. If we are going to have control over all this it must come from *outside* ourselves!

Cain couldn't stop either. Cain, you remember, was Adam and Eve's firstborn. Abel was Cain's younger brother. Cain kept the fields; Abel kept the sheep. And there was a growing conflict between the two of them because of a requirement from God. Cain was rejected; Abel was accepted. The hate in Cain's heart simmered and stewed. Then one day it boiled over.

> Now Cain said to his brother Abel, "Let's go out to the field." And while they were in the field, Cain attacked his brother Abel and killed him (Gen. 4:8, NIV).

Why? Because mentally, his mind was depraved. Emotionally, he was insanely jealous. Volitionally, he was defiant. Spiritually, he was dead. Physically, he carried his hatred to the extreme. Cain took a knife and slit the throat of his brother, as he had often seen Abel kill the sheep. He murdered his own brother in a cold-blooded act of rage . . . and he wasn't even remorseful about it.

I don't know if you watched the television docudrama some years back called *Into Thin Air*. It was the true account of a young Canadian collegian who decided to go to school in the United States. He drove the family Volkswagen van toward Colorado to begin his schooling. The family was a little concerned about the condition of the car and warned him that he might have some trouble. The young man seemed unconcerned about the problem as he kissed his family good-bye and sped off to school.

He vanished "into thin air." The parents became more than worried, because as time passed it was obvious that wrong had occurred. Ultimately, they were forced to believe their son must have been killed. Indeed he was. He had been murdered by two brutal men.

The murderers were finally caught. There is a gripping scene toward the end of this drama where one of the guilty murderers sits in the office of the FBI investigator. He's answering questions rather calmly during this interrogation. When he gets to the actual killing that he and his partner committed, it is incredible how cool his remarks seem.

He repeats a statement, "And so we killed him." There is a photographic flashback to the scene in the back of the van where the boy is face down on the floorboard, bound and gagged. Then you see the men as they drag the boy out into the snow. Back to the FBI room—"And so we killed him." Flashback: One man has a knife and stabs, stabs, stabs, stabs that knife into the chest of the boy. In the FBI room— "And so we killed him." Flashback: The scene is now on the slope of a snow-covered hill as they drag him to a rapid-moving stream and a waterfall where they dump his bloody body into the water. A crimson color fills the whole stream and his body bobs face down in the icy water. In the interrogation room—"And so we killed him . . . we killed him."

The common response when listening or watching such a

program is to think, "What a terrible man!" and to imagine, "How much better I am." No—wrong assumption. Before you resist that thought, remember you, too, are depraved. In the heart of every one of us is the same murderous nature. We may not stab with a hunting knife, but we stab with our vile tongues. We stab with our thoughts. We stab with our looks. We stab with our actions. We kill. We murder. We deceive. We deny. We reject. We kick. We batter. And all the while we ignore our depravity as we cluck our tongues at a man who says, "So we killed him."

It's only a difference of degrees. Except for the grace of God I could have confessed to the same thing. And so could you.

Why? Genesis 5:1,3:

> This is the book of the generations of Adam. In the day when God created man, He made him *in the likeness of God.* When Adam had lived one hundred and thirty years, he became the father of a son *in his own likeness,* according to his image, and named him Seth (emphasis mine).

Look! Verse 1: "... in the likeness of God," that's when God made Adam. A little later, " . . . in his own likeness," that's when Adam and Eve had a child. When Eve gave birth, it was in Adam's likeness, not God's. Why? Because depravity had flooded humanity and polluted the innocence. Sin intercepted the pass and it will *never* give the ball back—never! Not on this earth. The real tragedy is that the disease has spread to all mankind. It is not limited to the Old Testament. It is not limited to the family of Adam and Eve:

> What then? Are we better than they? Not at all; for we have already charged that both Jews and Greeks are all under sin; as it is written,
> There is none righteous, not even one;
> There is none who understands,
> There is none who seeks for God;
> All have turned aside, together they
> have become useless;
> There is none who does good,
> There is not even one.

Their throat is an open grave,
With their tongues they keep deceiving,
The poison of asps is under their lips;
Whose mouth is full of cursing and bitterness
Their feet are swift to shed blood,
Destruction and misery are in their paths,
And the path of peace have they not known.
There is no fear of God before their eyes (Rom. 3:9-18).

I can imagine a cartoon that might appear in some business magazine, showing a tired business man late one evening—tie pulled loose after a busy day—watching a business report. Only this time things are much more realistic. Imagine his startled look as he hears:

Closing averages in the human scene were mixed today:
- Brotherly Love—down a couple of points.
- Self-interest—up a half.
- Vanity showed no movement.
- Guarded Optimism—slipped a point in the sluggish trading.

Overall, really nothing changed."

The guy would probably blink in amazement, but he would have no reason to be that surprised. After all, he is a student of humanity. He knows in his heart that "really nothing changed." Depravity is monotonously predictable.

Therefore, just as through one man sin entered into the world, and death through sin, and so death spread to all men, because all sinned (5:12).

Think of it this way: There is a king named Sin; there is a queen named Death. Both of them rule over mankind—"so death spread to all men, because all sinned."

Extending Your Roots

1. Cain, son of Adam and Eve, was mentally depraved. Emotionally, he was insanely jealous. Jealousy, envy, and

hatred are sins because these are motives for murder whether one murders or not. Read Genesis 4 to trace the development of jealousy. Write your discovery below:
How jealousy develops:

How jealousy can be overcome:

What is the outcome of unresolved jealousy:

2. Identify how negative attitudes can hinder *your* relationship with God and with others.

3. Pray silently about any personal attitude that has the potential for sinning.

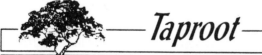 *Taproot*

1. Adam and Eve are the first couple and parents mentioned in Genesis. Cain and Abel are the first siblings. Using the letters in the word *family*, fill in the following acrostic with words describing this first family.

F
A
M
I
L
Y

2. Depravity is not limited to the family of Adam and Eve. Use the following acrostic to list words describing a contemporary family.

F

A

M

I

L

Y

3. Now look at an example of a healthy family. Read Luke 2:41-51. Complete the acrostic with words describing this family.

F

A

M

I

L

Y

4. Finally, think about your family. Write words that reflect family life in your home.

F

A

M

I

L

Y

If words like *fighting, anger, meanness, inconsiderate, lying,* and *yelling* are listed, what can you do to correct this trend toward depravity?

5 What It All Means . . . Personally

Now here's our problem. We suffer from the very same disease as did Adam, Eve, Cain—you name 'em. This Book called the Bible may be old, but it isn't out of date. It may tell us our story in ancient terms, but its message is still true, still relevant. We've got the disease, the same root problem—*depravity*.

And that root problem yields fruit—*sinfulness*—sinful thoughts, sinful words, sinful actions. There is nobody on earth who can help us! We're not unlike an egg named Humpty Dumpty:

> Humpty Dumpty sat on a wall.
> Humpty Dumpty had a great fall;
> All the king's horses
> And all the king's men
> Couldn't put Humpty Dumpty together again.

I was thinking about that not long ago (to give you some idea of the depth of my thoughts) and decided to go down to the library and do some study on Humpty Dumpty.

I will never forget the librarian's face when I asked, "Have you anything in the research stacks on Humpty Dumpty?" She just stared at me. So I thought I'd put it another way, "How about something on the etymology of Humpty?" That didn't help either.

Even though she couldn't help me, I managed to find some interesting things. I found that the little rhyme was never connected with an egg, not originally. That was added later. I discovered that Humpty Dumpty was perhaps originated by a rather creative teacher in the colonial days of our United States when children sat on hard oak benches and learned their ABCs. My reason for suggesting this is based on what I found in the New England Primer. In the Primer is this quaint couplet, not unlike Humpty Dumpty, that reads,

In Adam's fall
We sinned all.
Xerxes the Great did die,
And so must you and I.

It was used to teach children the letters "A" and "X." Who knows but what some teacher thought of a rhyme that would teach even more letters, for after all, "King Sin" and "Queen Death" still reigned in the seventeenth and eighteenth centuries.

We need help. We need somebody to put us together again. Romans 5:17 announces there *is* Someone!

For if, by the trespass of the one man, death reigned through that one man, how much more will those who receive God's abundant provision of grace and of the gift of righteousness reign in life through the one man, Jesus Christ (NIV).

Isn't that good news? There is Someone to whom we can turn. You won't find anybody on earth who qualifies as a sinless sacrifice. Being such a sacrifice requires perfection. That's why He was virgin born. God intercepted the birth process and placed in Mary's womb the embryo perfectly designed to provide the sinless sacrifice . . . the Lamb of God who would take away the sin of the world. After living a perfect life, He went to the cross where He satisfied—once for all—the righteous demands of a holy God against sin.

Even though "we sinned all," thanks to Adam . . . even though "Xerxes the Great did die, and so must you and I," Christ is our hope. He came to our rescue. He saw us in our depravity, He heard our confession of need, He gave us the hope of forgiveness.

So let me close with my own revised edition of Humpty Dumpty.

Jesus Christ came to our wall;
Jesus Christ died for our fall.
He slew Queen Death.
He crushed King Sin.
Through grace He put us together again.

The best part of all? "He put us together again." He picked up the pieces. He unscrambled the egg. To change the terms of the philosopher; wherever there is sin, there must have been a preceding sinner. And wherever there is a sinner, there must be a Savior.

And there is.

Extending Your Roots

1. Adam and Eve and Cain suffered from a root problem called *depravity*. The bad news is we inherited the disease. Our lives sometimes look like Humpty Dumpty at the bottom of the wall. How do we get back together again? How has sin separated you from God?

2. How can you avoid letting sin separate you from God?

3. What has God done to "put us back together again."

Growing Deep in the Christian Life: Salvation

Taproot

The Letter of 1 John is about love—a glue for mending depravity cracks.

1. Read 1 John 3:11-15. Not only should hate not be a part of your life, but you need to develop _____ for other people.

2. Read 1 John 4:19-20 to discover how to love others no matter what the circumstance.

3. Write a paraphrase of verse 20. Has God unscrambled your depravity?

6 Exposing the Dark Side

I like good news. Therefore, I prefer to emphasize the happy, bright, colorful side of life. But my problem with that emphasis is this: That is only *half* the message of Christianity. When we stop to think about it, we really cannot appreciate the bright and beautiful side of life until we know how dark and dismal the backdrop is. So, to be true to my calling and to be complete in this presentation of biblical doctrine, it is necessary to expose, along with the bright side of life, the dark side.

Back in 1886 Robert Louis Stevenson wrote a classic story that exposed everybody's life. He called it *Dr. Jekyll and Mr. Hyde*. Although a little older, Stevenson was a contemporary of Mark Twain, the American storyteller. And perhaps it was from that story that Twain came up with the statement so familiar to all of us: "Everybody is a moon; and has a dark side which he never shows to anybody."[1]

No one ever said it better than Jesus when He spoke so sternly against the hypocrisy of the Pharisees and scribes.

> Woe to you, scribes and Pharisees, hypocrites! For you are like whitewashed tombs which on the outside appear beautiful, but inside they are full of dead men's bones and all uncleanness. Even so you too outwardly appear righteous to men, but inwardly you are full of hypocrisy and lawlessness (Matt. 23:27-28).

Lest you live under the delusion that the "dark side" was a problem only former generations struggled with, just think about your life over the past several days. Think inwardly rather than outwardly. More than likely you behaved yourself rather well externally . . . but not from within! Call to mind the impulses, the drives, the secrets, the motives behind the actions you lived out. Perhaps a few of them did surface, but most of your dark side remained hidden to the public. French essayist Michel De Montaigne put it this way:

> There is no man so good, who, were he to submit all his thoughts and actions to the laws, would not deserve hanging ten times in his life.[2]

Depravity Defined and Explained

It's helpful to remember that the deadliest killer of humanity is not heart disease or cancer . . . it is depravity, our most ancient and all-pervasive disease. Every one of us has it. Every one of us suffers from the consequences of it. And to make matters even worse, we pass it on to each new generation. As we learned earlier, it has "spread to all men."

One of the most sweeping, broad-brush statements in all of Scripture on the depravity of humanity is found in Genesis 6:5:

> Then the Lord saw that the wickedness of man was great on the earth, and that every intent of the thoughts of his heart was only evil continually.

Are you as gripped as I am when I read three words in that verse? Look at them again: "every," "only," "continually." The scene described in this verse is an inescapable, universal cesspool in the inner person of all humanity—a hidden source of pollution that lies at the root of wrong. Even from childhood this is true.

A number of years ago the Minnesota Crime Commission released this statement:

> Every baby starts life as a little savage. He is completely selfish and self-centered. He wants what he wants when he wants it—his bottle, his mother's attention, his playmates' toy, his uncle's watch. Deny him these once, and he seethes

with rage and aggressiveness, which would be murderous were he not so helpless. He is in fact, dirty. He has no morals, no knowledge, no skills. This means that all children—not just certain children—are born delinquent. If permitted to continue in the self-centered world of his infancy, given free reign to his impulsive actions to satisfy his wants, every child would grow up a criminal—a thief, a killer, or a rapist.

Now that's reality. And if it's your tendency as a positive thinker to ignore it, it still won't go away. If it's your tendency as a parent to ignore it, that root of depravity will come back to haunt you in your home. A permissive, think-only-about-the-bright-side-of-life philosophy will be eaten alive by problems of depravity as your child grows up without restraints and without controls. Not even a kind and professional Dr. Jekyll could remove the savage-like Mr. Hyde from his own life. Face it, the dark side is here to stay.

Psalm 51 is another section of Scripture worth examining as we come to terms with depravity. It is the psalm David wrote following Nathan's confrontation with him after the adultery-murder-hypocrisy scandal.

> Be gracious to me, O God, according to Thy lovingkindness; according to the greatness of Thy compassion blot out my transgressions. Wash me thoroughly from my iniquity, and cleanse me from my sin. For I know my transgressions, and my sin is ever before me. Against Thee, Thee only, I have sinned, and done what is evil in Thy sight, so that Thou art justified when Thou dost speak, and blameless when Thou dost judge. Behold, I was brought forth in iniquity, and in sin my mother conceived me (vv. 1-5).

He begins with a plea for grace, which shouldn't surprise us. The only way David could expect to survive would be by the grace of God. That's the reason *any* of us survive! What is grace? How would you define it? Probably, the most popular two-word definition is "unmerited favor." To amplify that a bit: Grace is what God does for humankind, which we do not deserve, which we cannot earn, and which we will never be able to repay. Awash in our sinfulness, helpless to change on our own, polluted to the core with no possibility of cleaning ourselves up, we cry out for grace. It is our only hope.

That's why David's prayer begins, "Be gracious." He doesn't deserve God's favor. He's fallen into sin. His life is a mess. So he asks that God would be gracious according to His lovingkindness.

Following his unguarded, open confession, David addresses the nucleus of his problem. He was "brought forth in iniquity" because his mother conceived him "in sin." He doesn't mean that the act of conception was sinful. *The Amplified Bible* handles the meaning quite well:

> Behold, I was brought forth in [a state of] iniquity; my mother was sinful who conceived me [and I, too, am sinful].

"I have come from sinful parents, and therefore I have had the same disease passed on to me—so please be gracious to me, O God." That's the idea.

Lest we feel a little smug, thinking that David was all alone in the struggle against sin, let's return to the Jekyll-and-Hyde reminder . . . we've *all* got the disease. Depravity affects all of us. Because Adam fell, we, too, fell. Theologian Dwight Pentecost addresses the issue of Adam's fall. Read his words carefully:

> One of the most important questions which you can face is the question, "How far did Adam fall?" A number of different answers have been given to that question.
> The liberal says that Adam fell upward, so that Adam's lot was better after the fall than before the fall because something was added to the personality of Adam of which he had been deprived previously. Consequently, Adam was a fuller and more complete person after the fall than he was before the fall. There are those who say that when Adam fell, he fell over the cliff, but that when he was going over the cliff he grabbed something on the top of the cliff and held on. He fell downward, but he held on before he slipped over the brink, and if he exerts enough will and enough strength he can pull himself back up over the brink and stand on solid ground

again. Those who have that concept are trying to lift themselves by their own bootstraps and work their way into heaven.

Then, there is the teaching that says that when Adam fell, he slipped over the brink but he landed on a ledge part way down and that the ledge is the church and the church will lift him up and put him on solid ground again.

But the Word of God says that when Adam fell he fell all the way. He became depraved, totally depraved, unable to do anything to please God. He is under sin, dead, under judgment, under Satan's control; he is lost.[3]

Extending Your Roots

Dr. Jekyll was a dignified gentleman raised in Victorian England. He had a strict sense of what was right and wrong. However, an evil impulse tormented him. The doctor sometimes became a totally different person by drinking a chemical solution. As you know, the good doctor's experiment failed. Light and dark do not mix.

1. The apostle Paul had an experience as a Christian struggling against sin. Read Romans 7:15-25. If your Bible has cross-references, read all the references suggested in this passage of Scripture.

2. Describe a present-day Christian battling good and evil in his or her life.

Taproot

Sooner or later you will experience "dark side" behavior just like Paul. On a scale of 1 to 10, with 1 representing the dark side of your life and 10 representing the light side of your life, circle the number which describes your behavior in the following situations.

A person of another race or culture moves into your neighborhood.

1 2 3 4 5 6 7 8 9 10

An extended family member receives an unexpected salary increase.

1 2 3 4 5 6 7 8 9 10

A person you really dislike is diagnosed with a terminal disease.

1 2 3 4 5 6 7 8 9 10

The pastor of a successful, growing church in your community is caught in a moral sin.

1 2 3 4 5 6 7 8 9 10

Your friend's son is accepted into your alma mater; your daughter is rejected.

1 2 3 4 5 6 7 8 9 10

A person with HIV joins your church.

1 2 3 4 5 6 7 8 9 10

Do you have any secrets? Any dark sides?

7 Humanity Surveyed and Exposed

One of the wonderful things about the Bible, which only adds to its credibility, is that it tells us the truth, the whole truth, and nothing but the truth regarding its characters. I often say it doesn't airbrush the pen portraits. When it paints its heroes, it paints them warts and all. The scars are not hidden. And about the time you're tempted to elevate certain men and women in Scripture to a pedestal of worship, God brings them down to size. Each one is completely, totally, and thoroughly H-U-M-A-N. They are all as James refers to Elijah: ". . . a man with a nature like ours" (Jas. 5:17).

Three Old Testament Characters

Noah

I'd like to introduce a man who first appears in Genesis, chapter 6. What a wonderful man he was! We need to be reminded of the times in which he lived. We just read about that awful scene in Genesis 6:5 as it described Noah's surroundings. The Lord said that He was grieved that He had even made mankind. And so before judging humanity with the flood, He surveyed the world, looking for one who would qualify as a righteous man. And He found one, only one, who found favor in His sight. His name was Noah.

> These are the records of the generations of Noah. Noah was a righteous man, blameless in his time; Noah walked with God (v. 9).

This verse says three things about Noah: He was "righteous," "blameless," and he "walked with God." That's quite a résumé! Here is a good man, surrounded by gross wickedness . . . a flower growing out of a cesspool. He was so good, God appointed him to build the ark and to save his family from death. And that's exactly what Noah did. He worked on it consistently for 120 years. And while he worked, he preached. And as he preached, he warned. And when he finished the ark, he got his family inside, though nobody else was interested, and the flood came. They alone were saved from destruction. It's one of those stories we never tire of hearing. And Noah comes out, of course, smelling like a rose. Public hero number one!

Chapter 9 brings us to the end of the flood and presents Noah and his family to a new earth.

Here stands a man who has been walking with God for all these years. What a model of courage and determination! But as we're about to fall on our knees to worship him we find he has feet of clay. Yes, even Noah. Unlike the moon, he is forced to show his dark side.

> Then Noah began farming and planted a vineyard. And he drank of the wine and became drunk, and uncovered himself inside his tent. And Ham, the father of Canaan, saw the nakedness of his father, and told his two brothers outside (vv. 20-22).

I don't pretend to know all that his uncovering himself implies. It was, no doubt, sexually perverse, because his sons were ashamed to be in his presence in his naked condition. On top of that, the man was drunk.

It seems amazing that a good man—so good he was picked above all other men—would get himself drunk in his tent and blatantly uncover himself. So wicked was Noah's disobedience that his sons were not only shamed by it, but cursed because of it. As in the case of Adam and Eve, a divine curse followed disobedience. It is like an instant replay. It's shocking if you forget that even in Noah there was a depraved nature.

Every now and then a once-great man or godly woman will fall. So great will be the fall that their defection will make headline attention in Christian and secular publications alike. Even though we know the doctrine of depravity, we're still stunned.

In one sense it is only natural to be surprised since we trusted the person to live obediently. In another sense we really have no reason to be shocked. Depravity affects us all—and even the so-called heroes of our life occasionally drop through the cracks. Before you become too disillusioned, remember Noah. Not even he was immune. Sometimes there is drunkenness, and sometimes there is sexual perversity. And when the truth comes out, our heroes die a painful death in our minds.

Learn a major lesson from this study: *No one on earth deserves your worship.* You tread on very thin ice when you enshrine any human individual—no matter how mightily he or she is being used of God.

Is it OK to have heroes? Sure it is. And it is certainly appropriate to respect them. But our respect should never come anywhere close to worship. When it does, and then your hero suddenly shows his weakness, you are going to be terribly disillusioned. It may not be as scandalous as it was with Noah, but they will fall in some way. They will show intemperance, or anger, or impatience, or even a lack of courtesy. If you get to know them well enough, you'll discover they're just people who have to put their britches on one leg at a time. Just like everyone else.

Try to remember that every person on earth is still a depraved human being. Some are being used by God, but in no way are they free from the disease. Example: Noah—a good man who distinguished himself in bad times, but was still imperfect.

Moses

The second man worth our consideration appears first on the pages of Scripture in Exodus, chapter 2. His name is Moses. I like Moses. So do you. Who wouldn't like Moses? He comes from an extremely humble origin. He very graciously handles his early successes. Hebrews 11 says that he refused to be called the son of Pharaoh's daughter. And finally, though he was well-educated, mighty in words and deeds, and considered by many to be the pharaoh-elect, he was a man who decided to serve the Lord, rather than himself. After a lengthy period of preparation he was used to lead the people through the wilderness. You probably know his story.

No other man in Scripture talked with God face to face. When Moses came down from the mountain, his face literally glowed with the Shekinah glory of Jehovah, having been in the presence of God. He was there when the finger of God drilled the Torah into stone. He came down from the mountain and presented the first copies of the written Word of God to the people of God. He oversaw the building of the tabernacle. He led a whole nation through the trackless deserts of the Sinai. He stayed faithfully by their side, though they often came at him with verbal guns blazing.

Now you'd think the man could virtually walk on water, but he couldn't. This same man, Moses, had a record of murder in his life. It occurred during his mid-life years.

> Now it came about in those days, when Moses had grown up, that he went out to his brethren and looked on their hard labors; and he saw an Egyptian beating a Hebrew, one of his brethren. So he looked this way and that, and when he saw there was no one around, he struck down the Egyptian and hid him in the sand (vv. 11-12).

Is that amazing? Well, not really, not if you believe in the depravity of humanity. In an unguarded moment, a moment of rash decision, Moses acted in the flesh as he killed an Egyptian. Yes, in a rage of anger he murdered him. And then tried to hide the evidence. Why? Because he knew he had done wrong.

Forty years later (aged eighty) he's out in the wilderness. He thinks he's going to be leading sheep for the rest of his life. And God steps on the scene and says, "You're the one I have chosen to lead My people out of Egypt." Now here is an eighty-year-old man with murder on his record. He knows that he has failed the Lord, and yet he hears God graciously coming back saying, "You are going to be My spokesman." You would think he would have learned enough to say right away, "Wherever You lead me, I will go." Does he do that? No.

Don't call Moses' response (recorded in Ex. 3:11 to 4:17) *humility*. It's stubbornness. It's willful resistance.

Moses also battled with a temper—a short fuse. It may have gotten a little longer the older he got, but he never fully conquered it. But those of us who are impatient can't afford to be too critical of Moses. We know what it is to fight a bad temper. We try many ways to keep the fuse wet. When it gets dry it tends to make everything explode. Moses is a man who had that problem. Why? Because he was depraved. He was a good man. He was a leader. He was God's spokesman. But he still had a depraved nature. A Mr. Hyde nature lived inside his Dr. Jekyll skin. You see him on display in these lines from Numbers 20:

> And there was no water for the congregation; and they assembled themselves against Moses and Aaron. The people thus contended with Moses and spoke, saying, "If only we had perished when our brothers perished before the Lord! Why then have you brought the Lord's assembly into this wilderness, for us and our beasts to die here? And why have you made us come up from Egypt, to bring us in to this wretched place? It is not a place of grain or figs or vines or pomegranates, nor is there water to drink." Then Moses and Aaron came in from the presence of the assembly to the doorway of the tent of meeting, and fell on their faces. Then the glory of the Lord appeared to them; and the Lord spoke to Moses, saying, "Take the rod; and you and your brother Aaron assemble the congregation and speak to the rock before their eyes, that it may yield its water. You shall thus bring forth water for them out of the rock and let the congregation and their beasts drink." So Moses took the rod from before the Lord, just as He had commanded him; and Moses and Aaron gathered the assembly before the rock. And he said to

them, "Listen now, you rebels; shall we bring forth water for you out of this rock? Then Moses lifted up his hand and struck the rock twice with his rod, and water came forth abundantly, and the congregation and their beasts drank. But the Lord said to Moses and Aaron, "Because you have not believed Me, to treat Me as holy in the sight of the sons of Israel, therefore you shall not bring this assembly into the land which I have given them" (vv. 2-12).

What a story! Many people see only judgment here. I see grace. Did you catch those words? "... and water came forth abundantly." If you had been God, would *you* have brought water out of the rock? No way. But grace brings water even when there's disobedience. Why would Moses, this good man, strike the rock, when God has just said, "Speak to it"? I'm going to repeat it until it sinks in: *Because he was depraved.* Color Moses blue. He had a dark side he didn't want anybody to see, but on this occasion it was on display.

Before you get too pious and judgmental with Moses, just think about the rods and rocks in your life. Call to mind a few of the times you knew what was best and you did what was worst—when you realized in your heart that patience pays off, yet you acted impatiently. Want to know why you did it? Because *you're* depraved. Because you too have a dark side. Maybe it's a temper. Maybe it's greed. Or gossip. Or lust. Or overeating or drugs and booze. It could be envy, jealousy, or a dozen other things I could name. We all have them and they are often our besetting sins. Depravity reveals itself in numerous ways—all of them dark.

David

Having looked at Noah and Moses, let's consider perhaps the most popular character in the Old Testament, the man after God's heart, King David. My favorite piece of sculpture is a work by Michelangelo, the statue of David—white marble, standing at the end of a long corridor in Florence, Italy. As you study the statue, you stand in awe, not only of an artist's ability with a mallet and chisel but of God's marvelous plan in taking a teenager from a flock of sheep owned by his father and bringing him to lead His people. A beautiful summary of his story appears in Psalm 78.

> He also chose David His servant, and took him from the sheepfolds; from the care of the ewes with suckling lambs He brought him, to shepherd Jacob His people, and Israel His inheritance. So he shepherded them according to the integrity of his heart, and guided them with his skillful hands (vv. 70-72).

But the earliest reference to David is found in 1 Samuel 13 as Samuel speaks to Saul—who has forfeited the right to rule the people.

> And Samuel said to Saul, "You have acted foolishly; you have not kept the commandment of the Lord your God, which He commanded you, for now the Lord would have established your kingdom over Israel forever. But now your kingdom shall not endure. The Lord has sought out for Himself *a man after His own heart* (vv. 13-14a, emphasis mine).

You could write in the margin of your Bible, "Reference to David." A man after the very heart of God. And David stays faithful to God for well over a dozen years while jealous Saul hunts him down.

Finally, David is given the throne of Israel. He takes a nation that's bottomed-out spiritually, militarily, and economically. He expands its boundaries from 6,000 to 60,000 square miles. He establishes trade routes with the world. He equips them with a respectable military fighting force. David literally puts the nation on the map. He gives Israel a flag that flies higher than it had ever flown before. What a leader. What a hero. What a man of battle. What a courageous, faithful man of God—"a man after His own heart."

If you're looking for somebody to respect as a leader in biblical days, you don't have to go much further than David. David proves himself to be a man who continues to walk with God as he leads the nation correctly and courageously.

Until you get to 2 Samuel, chapter 11.

Until you come to one particular evening.

As king, he should have been in battle with his troops.

Instead he was at ease in the palace. And that was how he happened to take a fateful walk on his roof.

Now when evening came David arose from his bed and walked around on the roof of the king's house, and from the roof he saw a woman bathing; and the woman was very beautiful in appearance. So David sent and inquired about the woman. And one said, "Is this not Bathsheba, the daughter of Eliam, the wife of Uriah the Hittite?" And David sent messengers and took her, and when she came to him, he lay with her; and when she had purified herself from her uncleanness, she returned to her house. And the woman conceived; and she sent and told David, and said, "I am pregnant" (vv. 2-5).

You know the rest of the tragic story. Not only had our hero been involved with another woman outside wedlock (he certainly didn't need another woman), he had now found himself in a place of intense compromise and pressure. The thought of abortion was never in their mind—certainly not. But she was pregnant with his child. In a state of panic, David realized he had to so something about her husband Uriah. He tried to mask the story. Brought the man back from battle. Hoped that he would sleep with his wife. But Uriah, more faithful to the cause of Israel than David was, refused. And finally, the king instructed Joab to put Uriah into the heat of the battle. When that happened, of course, Uriah was killed. Joab sent a messenger back, knowing the heart of his leader, and among other things, he said, "You be sure and tell King David that Uriah was killed." The deceptive plot thickened.

I ask you, how could a man as godly as David fall as far as he did with Bathsheba? How could he be responsible for murdering a man on the battlefield? How could he live the life of a hypocrite for almost a year? How could David do that? He's our hero! He's that faithful shepherd! He's the giant killer!

The answer is going to sound terribly familiar—he is depraved. He has a nature that will never improve. He has lust, just like every man and every woman reading these words right now. And he yielded to it. As lust played its sweet song, the king of Israel danced to the music. He was responsible, just as you and I are every time we yield. Like Noah and Moses, David's lapse into sin left him vulnerable to its consequences. When depravity wins a victory, many get hurt—not just the one who is most responsible. Never forget that!

Most of us have been down the pike far enough to know that we cannot trust our sinful nature. Heed this word of counsel: *Don't get yourself in a situation when your nature takes charge.* If you are weakened by lust when you are with the opposite sex, you have to keep yourself out of those tempting situations where you will yield. If you play around the fire, it is only a matter of time. It won't be "if" but "when." And make no mistake about it, it will be your fault because you played the fool. And I can assure you, others will be burned in the same fire.

It is terribly important, especially in the area of personal morality, that we keep a safe distance when there is the temptation to be involved in illicit activity. I hope you never forget this warning. We are living in a day when moral purity and marital infidelity are being rationalized and compromised. More and more people—more and more *Christians* —are convincing themselves it's OK to fudge a little.

If you're sleeping with somebody who is not your mate, you're in sin. You're displeasing God. If you're walking away from God in an area of sexual activity, it is hurting your testimony and hurting the ministry of Jesus Christ. Face the music and get back in step! Claim the grace that's coming to you through Christ. Say, as David finally said "I have sinned," and turn around. Do it now!

And may I add? If you are in ministry and doing that, clean up your life or get out of the ministry. Do everyone else in ministry a favor, if you refuse to repent just step out of the ministry and say, "I have sinned. I have forfeited the right to lead a flock. I've compromised. I've ruined my personal testimony, but I refuse to ruin the testimony of the church." Better still, return to the Lord and claim His forgiveness. Christ is coming back for His Bride, the church, expecting her to be pure, "having no spot or wrinkle or any such thing; but that she should be holy and blameless" (Eph. 5:27).

Two New Testament Characters

Before we wrap up this chapter, let's glance at a couple of New Testament heroes.

Peter

One of those heroes must surely be Peter! Remember his greatest moment with his fellow disciples and his Lord?

> Now when Jesus came into the district of Caesarea Philippi, He began asking His disciples, saying, "Who do people say that the Son of Man is?" And they said, "Some say John the Baptist; and others Elijah; but still others, Jeremiah, or one of the prophets." He said to them, "But who do you say that I am?" And Simon Peter answered and said, "Thou art the Christ, the Son of the living God" (Matt. 16:13-16).

What a grand statement of faith! Good for you, Peter! With boldness and uncompromising assurance, the man spoke the truth. His theology? Impeccable. His faith? Impressive. I think Jesus wanted to applaud him. He did, in effect, when He told him that flesh and blood hadn't revealed that to him. Peter's answer came from the very portals of heaven. "God revealed that to you, Peter." It was his moment.

A little later on, Peter is again with his Lord. And the Lord is telling him about the future.

> And Jesus said to them, "You will all fall away, because it is written, 'I will strike down the shepherd, and the sheep shall be scattered.' But after I have been raised, I will go before you to Galilee." But Peter said to Him, "Even though all may fall away, yet I will not" (Mark 14:17-29).

Now Peter meant well. I've said things like that, haven't you? In a moment of great emotional gush, Peter made

sweeping promises to his Lord. Reminds me of the standard New Year's resolution:
Journal Entry: January 1—I'll meet with You every day of this new year, Lord.
January 4—Lord, I've missed the last two days, but I'm back.
Let's not be too critical of Peter. The man meant it with all his heart.

> "Even though all may fall away, yet I will not." And Jesus said to him, "Truly I say to you, that you yourself this very night, before a cock crows twice, shall three times deny Me" (Mark 14:29,30).

And that's exactly what happened. The fact is, he later denied his Lord openly and unashamedly. How can it be that this sincere disciple who made such a right-on statement of faith could drift so far, so fast?

In the same chapter of Mark's Gospel, we find the same man masking his identity:

> But he [Peter] began to curse and swear, "I do not know this man [Jesus] you are talking about!" (v. 71).

Peter's "Mr. Hyde" was on display. A darkness so horrible we don't even want to imagine it. Peter, however, could never forget it.

And then we read:

> And immediately a cock crowed a second time. And Peter remembered how Jesus had made the remark to him, "Before a cock crows twice, you will deny Me three times." And he began to weep (v. 72).

I don't think there is any weeping as bitter as the weeping brought on by spiritual failure. It's downright terrible! I'm thinking of a minister friend of mine who has failed the Lord through sexual compromise. He has stepped away from leadership and ministry. His flock is still in shock. At this very moment he is going through the time of weeping, like Peter. He knows he has forfeited the right to lead. And now that he has repented and come clean, he realizes the heinous condition of his soul during that period of time when he was compromising. I met with him to encourage him. Several times he broke into audible sobs. Like Peter, he was weeping in anguish before God. He is now seeking God's will for his future.

Why did Peter do that? Why did my friend do that? I repeat, at the risk of sounding like a broken record, you and I are prone to wander, prone to leave the God we love *because of the depravity of humanity.*

Paul

Can it be that a man as fine as Paul would be included? Romans, chapter 7, I think, is the finest explanation of humanity's depraved nature found anywhere in the Scriptures. We've looked at Noah and Moses and David. In the New Testament we're looking at Peter and Paul. If I had time, I could also include Mary—Peter, Paul, and Mary (couldn't resist it). But we'll stop with Paul.

Listen to the personal testimony of a great man of God, the theologian par excellence, the missionary, the apostle, the founder of churches, the man who forged out the finer points of our theology, who wrote more of the New Testament than any other writer. Read Paul's admission slowly and thoughtfully:

> I do not understand what I do. For what I want to do I do not do, but what I hate I do. And if I do what I do not want to do, I agree that the law is good. As it is, it is no longer I myself who do it, but it is sin living in me. I know that nothing good lives in me, that is, in my sinful nature. For I have the desire to do what is good, but I cannot carry it out. For what I do is not the good I want to do; no, the evil I do not want to do—this I keep on doing. Now if I do what I do not want to do, it is no longer I who do it, but it is sin living in me that does it.
>
> So I find this law at work: When I want to do good, evil is right there with me. For in my inner being I delight in God's law; but I see another law at work in the members of my body, waging war against the law of my mind and making me a prisoner of the law of sin at work within my members.

What a wretched man I am! Who will rescue me from this body of death? (vv. 15-24, NIV).

I hardly need to amplify. Paul's testimony is everyone's testimony. That's why we sin. That's why the ark builder got drunk, why a leader lost his temper, why a king committed adultery, and why a disciple denied his Lord. Even though we wish to do good, evil is present in all of us. John R. W. Stott said it best:

> We human beings have both a unique dignity as creatures made in God's image and a unique depravity as sinners under his judgment. The former gives us hope; the latter places a limit on our expectations. Our Christian critique of the secular mind is that it tends to be either too naively optimistic or too negatively pessimistic in its estimates of the human condition, whereas the Christian mind, firmly rooted in biblical realism, both celebrates the glory and deplores the shame of our human being. We can behave like God in whose image we are made, only to descend to the level of the beasts. We are able to think, choose, create, love, and worship, but also to refuse to think, to choose evil, to destroy, to hate, and to worship ourselves. We build churches and drop bombs. We develop intensive care units for the critically ill and use the same technology to torture political enemies who presume to disagree with us. This is 'man,' a strange bewildering paradox, dust of earth and breath of God, shame and glory.[1]

Extending Your Roots

1. The doctrine of total depravity means that a person is lost and spiritually dead. It is not that a person is ignorant or requires instruction. The New Testament presents a rich young ruler who came to Jesus. Read Matthew 19:16-22; Mark 10:17-31; and Luke 18:18-30 and develop a profile of the LIGHT and DARK sides of this man's life.

Growing Deep in the Christian Life: Salvation

Light Side   Dark Side

2. What would you have said or done to lead the ruler to the LIGHT?

Many Bible people serve as examples of depravity. They responded to life in two ways: either the dark side or the light side. The following chart lists several individuals or groups who were very human. Sin was a problem for them. Select three names for a personal survey. Use a Bible concordance, Bible dictionary, and commentary as resources. Complete the information requested on the chart.

		Check one	
Biblical Person(s)	**Evidence of dark-side living**	**Found the light___**	**Depraved**
Absalom			
Gomer			
Samson			
Pharisees			
Israelites			
King Saul			
Lot			
The Samaritan woman			
Judas Iscariot			

1. How do you expose the dark side? Where is the light switch? In Psalm 51:1-17, we discover how King David came to terms with depravity. (For a refresher of the king's sin, read 2 Sam. 11.)

2. David confessed his dark side—his sin. He confessed. His confession to God included:
- recognition of God's willingness to forgive
- acknowledgment of his sin
- a plea for God's forgiveness
- acceptance of God's forgiveness.

Based on what you have learned from Psalm 51, write a brief paragraph describing how you can expose the dark side of your life.

 *Taproot*

3. How can you know if you are living on the light side? Several things indicate that you are. Check the statements that are part of your daily life.
- I read and study God's Word regularly.
- I apply what I read and study from the Bible to my life.
- I earnestly seek God's will for my life.
- My life reflects God's love.
- I serve God with my gifts and talents.
- I minister to the needs of others.
- I look for opportunities to witness for Jesus.
- I give at least a tithe to God.

Complete this checklist by writing beside each statement actual instances and experiences you have had this past month.

8 The One Great Exception

Jesus Christ is the exception—no shame in Him, only glory. No dark side, only light. No blue, only spotless white.

The Scripture says three things of Christ. He *knew* no sin; He *had* no sin; He *did* no sin. No sin nature. Born without sin. Lived without sinfulness. Knowing no sin, having no sin, doing no sin, He qualified as the Lamb of God who took away the power of sin and the dread of death. Therefore, when we confess our sins, He hears us and cleanses us. What a relief! We confess, "Guilty as charged." He answers, "Heard and forgiven!"

> And this is the message we have heard from Him and announce to you, that God is light, and in Him there is no darkness at all. If we say that we have fellowship with Him and yet walk in the darkness, we lie and do not practice the truth; but if we walk in the light as He Himself is in the light, we have fellowship with one another, and the blood of Jesus His Son cleanses us from all sin. If we say that we have no sin, we are deceiving ourselves, and the truth is not in us. If we confess our sins, He is faithful and righteous to forgive us our sins and to cleanse us from all unrighteousness (1 John 1:5-9).

Two Options—Choose One

When we boil these last few chapters down to basics, we really have two options. *First, we can choose to live as victims* of our depravity . . . for "evil is present in me," as Paul wrote. Or *second, we can choose to live as victors* through the power of Jesus Christ. The last thing I desire to do is to leave in your mind the impression that you must spend your years as a helpless, pitiful victim of depravity.

Each one of these people we've studied made a deliberate decision to sin. They weren't duped. It came as no sudden surprise. They played into the hand of the old nature, and they carried out exactly what the old nature performs . . . disobedience. They *chose* to live as victims, at least at that moment.

Let me encourage you to live as a victor through the power of Jesus Christ. Start by coming to the cross by faith. Ask Christ to come into your life. Then as you face evil, as you come across it, as it rears its head in temptation, claim the power of God that Christ offers, now that He's living within you.

You can say, "Lord, right now, at this moment, I am weak. You're strong. By your strength I'm stepping away from this evil, and Your power is going to give me the grace to get through it victoriously. Take charge right now." And walk away. Stand firm!

Remember the old gospel song "Just As I Am"? It is used at the close of every Billy Graham Crusade. While attending the crusade at Anaheim Stadium in 1985, I listened to that song night after night as thousands of people poured onto the playing field to turn their lives over to Jesus Christ. Some were lost; some were saved. But all sought help with the same problem—their sin. Only the Lamb of God can solve that problem.

> Just as I am, without one plea,
> But that Thy blood was shed for me,
> And that Thou bidd'st me come to Thee,
> O Lamb of God, I come! I come!
>
> Just as I am and waiting not
> To rid my soul of one dark blot,
> To Thee whose blood can cleanse each spot,
> O Lamb of God, I come! I come!

Just as I am, Thou wilt receive,
Wilt welcome, pardon, cleanse, relieve;
Because Thy promise I believe,
O Lamb of God, I come! I come![1]

Mr. Hyde has a greater bark than a bite. Trust me . . . no, trust God's Word. The Lord Jesus will help you face reality. He will see you through. Come to the Lamb of God. Hear again His promise of forgiveness.

Forgive us, Lord . . . for the things we have done that make us feel uncomfortable in Thy presence. All the front that we polish so carefully for me to see does not deceive Thee. For Thou knowest every thought that has left its shadow on our memory. Thou hast marked every motive that curdled something sweet within us.

We acknowledge—with bitterness and true repentance—that cross and selfish thoughts have entered our minds; we acknowledge that we have permitted our minds to wander through unclean and forbidden ways; we have toyed with that which we knew was not for us; we have desired that which we should not have.

We acknowledge that often we have deceived ourselves where our plain duty lay.

We confess before Thee that our ears are often deaf to the whisper of Thy call, our eyes often blind to the signs of Thy guidance.

Make us willing to be changed, even though it requires surgery of the soul and the therapy of discipline.

Make our hearts warm and soft, that we may receive now the blessing of Thy forgiveness, the benediction of Thy "Depart in peace . . . and sin no more." Amen.[2]

—Peter Marshall

1. Circle the word or phrase that most nearly describes your spiritual life right now:

excited and happy
dread each new day
really hurting
looking for meaning
prayerful
growing
borderline depraved
living in God's will

2. Study the Scripture passages listed below. Each one deals with a specific sin. As you read each chapter, decide if the people involved were victims or victors. At the conclusion of the study, answer the question about YOU truthfully.

The sin of idolatry
Exodus 32—34
Are you a victim of idolatry or a victor?

The sin of covetousness and disobedience
Joshua 8; 1 Samuel 15
Are you a victim of covetousness and disobedience?

The sin of hypocrisy and lying
Acts 5
Are you a victim or a victor of hypocrisy and lying?

The sin of pride
Luke 18:9-17
Are you a victim or victor of pride?

3. The one great exception to living on the dark side was the sinless Christ. This exceptional One wanted His followers to learn to live in the light. Throughout the Bible God is characterized as light, and sin is characterized as darkness. To understand this subject more fully, read each suggested Scripture passage from at least two Bible translations. Then use a commentary to read about the passage. The following chart will guide you in compiling your discoveries. Write in the left-hand column what you think the writer meant.

Write in the right hand column ways to apply this Scripture to your life in the light.

WHAT THE WRITER SAID   **APPLICATION**
1 John 1:5-10
John 1:9
John 8:1
John 3:19
2 Corinthians 6:14
Revelation 1:5
Romans 3:23

1. What are people saying about the light? The one great exception to depravity, Jesus Christ, wanted His disciples to answer that question for Him. So while walking along together, Jesus asked, "Who do people say that I am?"
List the three answers recorded in Mark 8:27-28:

2. The Light also wants to know what you are saying about Him. In the space provided, pretend you are telling a friend who lives in spiritual darkness about Jesus Christ, the Light of the world. What would you say about this sinless Savior?

3. Revelation 12:11 identifies how you can defeat Satan and depravity. Write the verse in this space.

4. Memorize one Scripture this week that assures you of victory over depravity.

Part

II

Salvation

9 "Mr. Smith, Meet Your Substitute"

When Peter Marshall preached, people listened. Even if they didn't believe what he said. Even when they said they were not interested. The man refused to be ignored.

Who can fully explain it? There was something about his winsome, contagious style that made it impossible for people not to listen. Even when he became the chaplain of the United States Senate and prayed more than he preached, his prayers became legendary. Ask those who were fortunate enough to have heard him. They'll tell you that everywhere Marshall preached, crowds gathered. Even if it were raining or snowing outside, the main floor and balconies would be full, packed with people, and many others who could not find a seat were willing to stand and listen as he spoke the truth of the living God.

Peter Marshall was Scottish, but his popularity went deeper than his Scottish brogue. And it certainly was more than just a charming personality or his well-timed humor that would win a hearing. The man had a way with men as well as with women. He was admired by both. A man's man and yet such a sensitive touch. At times one would swear he was more a poet than a preacher. He wasn't extemporaneous. To the surprise of many, Marshall *read* his sermons, considered a no-no by most professors of homiletics. But I suppose if one could read like Peter Marshall, who really cared if he broke that rule?

A contemporary of Marshall's said it best with this terse analysis:

> What Peter Marshall says, you never forget. . . . But it isn't *how* he says it, so much as *what* he says, you never forget. . . .

81

He has a gift for word pictures, for little dramas and folksy
incidents; he takes you out on the road to Galilee and makes
you think you belong there, and he brings you back sharply
to Main Street. He never preaches over your head.[1]

Perhaps that, more than any other single ingredient, was
the secret of the man's success. He certainly had the ability
to go much deeper, but he purposely restrained himself. He
was always cognizant of his audience. Since he was from an
impoverished background, he understood the common man
and woman. So he spoke in plain terms, colorful to be sure,
and dramatic at times; but people never had trouble con-
necting with what Peter Marshall was saying.

Listen to a part of one of his sermons:

> Our country is full of Joneses, and they all have problems
> of one kind or another. "All God's chillun' got trouble these
> days."
>
> The church has always contended that God can solve these
> problems through the individual's personal fellowship with
> a living Lord.
>
> Let's put the question bluntly, as bluntly as Mr. Jones
> would put it.
>
> Can you and I really have communion with Christ as we
> would with earthly friends?
>
> Can we know personally the same Jesus whose words are
> recorded in the New Testament, Who walked the dusty trails
> of Galilee two thousand years ago?
> I don't mean can we treasure His words
> or try to follow His example
> or imagine Him.
> I mean, is He really alive?
> Can we actually meet Him,
> communicate with Him,
> ask His help for our everyday affairs?
> The Gospel writers say "yes."
> A host of men and women down the ages say "yes."
> And the church says "yes."[2]

Appropriately, he entitled that sermon "Mr. Jones, Meet

the Master." I have hitchhiked on the man's idea by choosing a similar title for this chapter: "Mr. Smith, Meet Your Substitute." I figure that Mr. Jones has been picked on long enough. We need to give Jones a break. So, Mr. Smith, this is for you, as well as for your wife, and the Johnsons, the Franklins, the Clarks, the Parkers, or whatever your name may be. Because I'm writing to the common man and woman today who happens to find himself or herself in the same precarious predicament.

The predicament is called sin. And that's why you need a substitute.

Root Issues

1. I can vividly recall conversations with individuals who resisted the idea that they needed a Savior. Instead, they pointed out to me all the good things they had been "doing," feeling that it would "balance out on the scales" when they stood before God. How might you respond to that line of reasoning? To what Scripture might you direct such an individual? What illustrations could you use to help him or her get a grasp on the central truth of this chapter?

2. Become familiar with a simple gospel presentation that clearly illustrates how we cannot reach God through our own efforts. Booklets such as *Steps to Peace with God*, *The Four Spiritual Laws*, and *The Bridge to Life* are good examples. Choose one and buy several copies —keeping one handy in your wallet, pocket, or purse. You might meet a Mr. Smith or Miss Smith this week who needs to meet the Substitute.

3. I'll quote a bit from Romans 3 and 4 in this part of our study. Carve out some time this week to get a feel for this liberating portion of Scripture. Read Romans 3—5, preferably in two different translations of Scripture, if you have them. Reading these verses in either *The Living Bible* or

The New Testament in Modern English (Phillips) is an added treat. Ask the Lord to give you fresh insight as you trace this all important faith-root.

4. Read, contemplate, and *personalize* Isaiah 53 in a good paraphrase, such as *The Living Bible.* Can you visualize the Lord Jesus being crushed and weighed down by *your* sins? Find an "alone place" . . . an unhurried moment . . . and thank Him for dying for you so that you can experience daily "newness of life" (Rom. 6:4).

5. Imagine the kind of letter you might write to someone who had risked his or her own life to plunge into a swollen river and rescue you from drowning. Have you ever taken time to thank the Lord Jesus for literally laying down His life so that you could experience salvation and eternal life? Knock the rust off of your pen once again, open up your notebook, and write a letter of heartfelt gratitude and praise to your Savior for what He did for *you.*

6. Are there any "symbols" in your home—perhaps a cross, a figurine, a family Bible, or an artist's conception of Jesus that might draw away the adoration, attention, and honor that belongs to the Lord alone? Make a careful evaluation and deal decisively with that which could potentially become a stumbling block to you.

Extending Your Roots

Remembering can bring pain, laughter, sorrow, or regrets. Use the following phrases to practice the art of remembering *why* you need a substitute for your predicament of sin.

1. Write a brief phrase that describes your feelings at:
• a time when you experienced God's forgiveness

• a time when you failed God

- a time when you kept silent instead of witnessing about Christ

- a time when following God was too difficult

- a time when Sunday worship was inconvenient

- a time when you prayed once a week or less

2. Write a brief summary statement of your understanding about the need for a substitute for sin.

Taproot

1. Using a Bible paraphrase, such as *The Living Bible*, read the song of Moses in Deuteronomy 32:1-43. Underline Israel's sins. Compare these sins to contemporary sins.

2. Focus on verse 15. Read this verse from a commentary. Was the "Rock of their salvation" a substitute?

3. Have you met your Substitute?

10 Four Major Issues

Let's talk about the "why" issue.

The sixth book in the New Testament is the Book of Romans. In the third chapter of that book (which is actually a letter originally written to some people who lived in Rome, Italy, in the first century), you may be surprised to hear that *your* biography is included. It doesn't actually include your name or your place of residence, but it does tell the story of your personal life. The stuff it mentions isn't very attractive, I should warn you, but it is the truth. And so, Mr. Smith, this is your life. I mentioned it earlier, but it bears repeating.

Our Condition: Totally Depraved

What then? Are we better than they? Not at all; for we have already charged that both Jews and Greeks are all under sin; as it is written,
"There is none righteous, not even one;
There is none who understands,
There is none who seeks for God;
All have turned aside, together they have
become useless;
There is none who does good,
There is not even one."
"Their throat is an open grave,
With their tongues they keep deceiving."
"The poison of asps is under their lips";
"Whose mouth is full of cursing and bitterness";
"Their feet are swift to shed blood,
Destruction and misery are in their paths,

And the path of peace have they not known."
"There is no fear of God before their eyes."
Now we know that whatever the Law says, it speaks to those who are under the Law, that every mouth may be closed, and all the world may become accountable to God; because by the works of the Law no flesh will be justified in His sight; for through the Law comes the knowledge of sin. For all have sinned and fall short of the glory of God (Rom. 3:9-20, 23).

Honestly, now, does that sound like your life? Is that a fairly apt description of the inner you . . . down inside where nobody else can look? I think so. How do I know? Because it describes me, too. To borrow from my earlier comment, you and I are "blue all over." Even when we try to hide it, even when we put on our sophisticated best, it comes out when we least expect it.

Maybe you heard about the large commercial jet that was flying from Chicago to Los Angeles. About a half hour after takeoff, the passengers on board heard a voice over the loud speaker. "Good morning, ladies and gentlemen. This is a recording. You have the privilege of being on the first wholly electronically controlled jet. This plane took off electronically. It will soon be flying at 30,000 feet electronically. It will ultimately land electronically in Los Angeles. This plane has no pilot or copilot and no flight engineer because they are no longer needed. But do not worry, nothing can possibly go wrong, go wrong, go wrong, go wrong, go wrong, go wrong. . . ."

God's Character: Infinitely Holy

Next, my friend Smith, I should mention something that will only add insult to injury. God is righteous, perfect, and infinitely holy. That's His standard. It is sometimes called "glory" in the New Testament. We looked earlier at Romans 3:23. Let me paraphrase it:

For all have sinned [that's our condition] and fall short of the perfection, holiness, righteousness, and glory [that's His standard] of God.

88

Unlike all humanity, God operates from a different level
of expectation. His existence is in the realm of absolute perfection. He requires the same from others. Whoever hopes
to relate to Him must be as righteous as He is righteous.
How different from us! To relate to me you don't have to be
perfect. In fact, if you act like you are, I get very uncomfortable. "Just be what you are," we say. But God is not like
that. God doesn't shrug, wink, and say, "Ah, that's OK."

Let me put it another way. God's triangle is perfect. And
in order for you and me to fellowship with Him, our trian-
gles must be congruent. The sides and the angles must
match. So must the space within. Perfection requires
matching perfection.

Ah, there's the rub! We have sinned and fallen short of
the perfection of God. No one qualifies as perfect. Don't misunderstand, there are times that our goodness is astound-
ing. We take great strides, we produce great achievements.
We may even surprise ourselves with periodic times of goodness, gentleness, and compassion. But "perfect"? Never. Or
"infinitely holy"? How about "pure"? No, only God is those
things. Romans 3:21 calls God's perfection, holiness, and purity "The righteousness of God has been manifested, being
witnessed by the Law and the Prophets." Compared to *that*
standard, all humans come up short.

The New Testament in Modern English puts it like this:

> Iindeed it is the straight-edge of the Law that shows us
> how crooked we are (v. 20, Phillips).

Isn't that the truth? He is perfect and spotless white. Not a
taint of gray. Not a hint of blue. And along comes our blue
rectangle, trying to work its way into that perfect, holy, and
pure triangle. And the two just won't match! There is no
way, Mr. Smith, that we can match His righteousness.

Our Need: A Substitute

Here we are, sinners by birth, sinners by nature, sinners
by choice, trying to reach and attain a relationship with the
holy God who made us. And we "fall short." We can't make

it because we're spiritually crippled. In fact, the New Testament teaches us that we're "dead in trespasses and sin." What do we need? Let me put it plain and simple, Mr. Smith: we need help outside ourselves.

We need some way to become clean within so that we can relate to a God who is perfect. Scripture says, "God is light, and in Him there is no darkness at all" (1 John 1:5). If we hope to know God and walk with God and relate to God, we must be able to stand the scrutiny of that kind of light. But our light is out. We're all dark and He is all light. In his immortal hymn, Charles Wesley envisioned us in a dark dungeon, chained and helpless—

Long my imprisoned spirit lay
Fast bound in sin and nature's night.[1]

We can't get out of the dungeon, not even if we try. Our own sin holds us in bondage. We need someone to rescue us from the hole. We need an advocate in the courtroom of justice. We need someone who will present our case. We need someone to be our substitute. So God provided the Savior.

God's Provision: A Savior

. . . and are justified freely by his grace through the redemption that came by Christ Jesus. God presented him as a sacrifice of atonement, through faith in his blood. He did this to demonstrate his justice, because in his forbearance he had left the sins committed beforehand unpunished—he did it to demonstrate his justice at the present time, so as to be just and the one who justifies those who have faith in Jesus (vv. 24-26, NIV).

Is that great news? Mr. Smith, you have just been introduced to your substitute. He is Christ, the sinless and perfect Son of God. He is the One who accomplished your rescue. It occurred on a cross. It was effective because He was the only One who could qualify as our substitute before God. Sin requires a penalty—death—in order for God's righteous demands to be satisfied. The ransom must be paid. And Christ fills that role to perfection. You and I need to be washed. We need to be made sparkling clean. And God can't give up on His plan, for He hates sin. Being perfect He cannot relate to sinful things. He couldn't even if He tried, because His nature is repelled by sin. Sin calls for judgment. And that is why the cross is so significant. It becomes the place of judgment. It was there the price was paid in full.

In verse 24, the term *justified* appears. Let's work with that word a few moments. It does not simply mean "just as if I'd never sinned." That doesn't go far enough! Neither does it mean that God makes me righteous so that I never sin again. It means to be "declared righteous." Justification is God's merciful act, whereby He declares righteous the believing sinner while he is still in his sinning state. He sees us in our need, wallowing around in the swamp of our sin. He sees us looking to Jesus Christ and trusting Him completely by faith, to cleanse us from our sin. And though we come to Him with all of our needs and in all of our darkness, God says to us, "Declared righteous! Forgiven! Pardoned!" Wesley caught the significance of all this as he completed that same stanza:

Thine eye diffused a quick'ning ray,
I woke, the dungeon flamed with light;
My chains fell off, my heart was free;
I rose, went forth and followed Thee.[2]

I like the way Billy Graham imagines all this in a courtroom scene:

Picture a courtroom. God the Judge is seated in the judge's seat, robed in splendor. You are arraigned before Him. He looks at you in terms of His own righteous nature as it is expressed in the moral law. He speaks to you:

GOD: John (or) Mary, have you loved Me with all your heart?

JOHN/MARY: No, Your Honor.

GOD: Have you loved others as you have loved yourself?

JOHN/MARY: No, Your Honor.

GOD: Do you believe you are a sinner and that Jesus Christ died for your sins?

JOHN/MARY: Yes, Your Honor.

GOD: Then your penalty has been paid by Jesus Christ on the cross and you are pardoned. . . . Because Christ is righteous, and you believe in Christ, I now declare you legally righteous. . . .

Can you imagine what a newspaperman would do with this event?

SINNER PARDONED—
GOES TO LIVE WITH JUDGE

It was a tense scene when John and Mary stood before the Judge and had the list of charges read against them. However, the Judge transferred all of the guilt to Jesus Christ, who died on a cross for John and Mary.

After John and Mary were pardoned the Judge invited them to come to live with Him forever.

The reporter on a story like that would never be able to understand the irony of such a scene, unless he had been introduced to the Judge beforehand and knew His character.

Pardon and Christ's righteousness come to us only when we totally trust ourselves to Jesus as our Lord and Savior. When we do this, God welcomes us into His intimate favor. Clothed in Christ's righteousness we can now enjoy God's fellowship.[3]

All of that is included in what it means to be "justified." I come to Him in all my need. I am hopelessly lost, spiritually dead. And I present myself to Christ just as I am. I have nothing to give that would earn my way in. If I could I would, but I can't. So the only way I can present myself to Him in my lost condition is by faith. Coming in my need, expressing faith in His Son who died for me, I understand that God sees me coming by faith and admitting my sinfulness. At that epochal moment, He declares me righteous.

On occasion I think of the cross as a sponge . . . a "spiritual sponge" that has taken the sins of mankind—past, present, and future—and absorbed them all. At one awful moment, Christ bore our sins, thus satisfying the righteous demands of the Father, completely and instantaneously clearing up my debt. My sin is forgiven. My enslavement is broken. I am set free from sin's power over me once and for all. "Redemption," another significant word in verse 24, also occurs. I am set at liberty, so as never to come back to the slave market of sin—never again in bondage to it. And remember, the rescue occurred because of what *Christ* did—not because of what I did!

I love the way Romans 3:28 reads:

> For we maintain that a man is justified by faith apart from works of the Law.

I remember hearing a seasoned Bible teacher say, "Man is incurably addicted to doing something for his own salvation." What a waste! Scripture teaches that salvation is a by-faith, not-by-works transaction.

In Romans 4:4-5, this is made ever so clear:

> Now to the one who works, his wage is not reckoned as a favor, but as what is due. But to the one who does not work, but believes in Him who justifies the ungodly, his faith is reckoned as righteousness.

Just think of your paycheck, Mr. Smith. When your boss or someone from your boss's office brings you your paycheck, you take it. You take it, I might add, without a great deal of gratitude. You don't drop to your knees and say, "Oh, thank you—thank you so very much for this gift." You probably grab the check and don't give much thought to saying thanks. Why? Because you *earned* it. You worked *hard* for it. Now, if your boss attaches a bonus of a thousand bucks (and maybe even adds, "Though you're dropping in your efficiency, I want you to know I love you), wouldn't that be great? Great? That would be a miracle! There's a lot of difference between a wage and a gift.

God looks at us in all of our need and He sees nothing worth commending. Not only are we dropping in our spiritual efficiency, we have no light, no holiness. We're moving in the opposite direction, despising Him, living in a dungeon of sin, habitually carrying out the life-style of our sinful nature. Realizing our need, we accept His miraculous, eternal bonus—the gift of His Son. And in grace, our dungeon "flamed with light." You and I didn't even deserve the light, yet He gave it to us as an unmerited gift. Look again at verse 5:

> But to the one who does not work, but believes in Him who justifies the ungodly, his faith is reckoned as righteousness.

I love that verse! Because there's no way you and I can get any credit. We're bound in a dungeon, lost in ourselves. We don't even know where to find the light. Even when we try, we are like the title of the country-western song, "Looking for Love in All the Wrong Places."

Reminds me of the story I read recently about a drunk down on all fours late one night under a street light. He was groping around on the ground, feeling the cement, peering intently at the little cracks. And a friend drives up and says, "Sam, what are you doing there?" Sam answers, "I lost my wallet." So the friend gets out of his car, walks over, gets down on his hands and knees with him, and they both start looking. Neither one can find it. Finally the friend says to the drunk buddy:

> "Are you sure you lost the wallet here?"
> "Of course not! I dropped it half a block over there."
> "Then why are we looking here?"
> "Because there's no *streetlight* over there."

Mr. Smith, I'm going to level with you. I know you fairly well, even though we've never met. You read these words about the *gift* of eternal life and you simply cannot fathom them, so you won't take them. I mean, you've got your pride so you will reject them. I can even imagine your reluctance: "Too good to be true, Chuck. Sounds great. Looks good in a book. And it's definitely an intriguing idea. Who wouldn't want to tell people that? But if I get into heaven, I'll earn it on my own."

Well, let me give you just a little logic to wrestle with. If you plan to work your way in, how much work is enough work to guarantee that you have made it? And if it's something you work for, why does God say in His Book that it's for "the one who does *not* work, but believes"? Let me spell it out:

God's Character: infinitely holy
Our Condition: totally depraved
Our Need: a Substitute
God's Provision: a Savior

When God provided the Savior, He said to each one of us, "Here is My Gift to you." How often, when folks hear that, they shake their heads and mumble, "I can't believe it."

In 2 Corinthians 5:20, we find these words:

> Therefore, we are ambassadors for Christ, as though God were entreating through us; we beg you on behalf of Christ, be reconciled to God.

That's the message of this chapter in a nutshell. I beg you . . . be reconciled to God. Watch that barrier crumble, the one between you and God, as you step across by faith. Look at the next verse.

> He made Him who knew no sin to be sin on our behalf, that we might become the righteousness of God in Him (v. 21).

Now, let me identify the pronouns:

> He [God, the Father] made Him [God, the Son] who knew no sin to be sin on our behalf [that happened at the cross], that we [the sinner] might become the righteousness of God in Him [Christ].

Let's boil it down:
God: the righteous
Christ: the sacrifice
We: the sinner
Christ: the life
How? The cross.

But how can the sinner in the black hole of his need ever know God in the spotless white of all of His righteousness? Verse 20 tells us. By coming to know Him who knew no sin, the one who became sin on our behalf. Put your pride in your pocket, Mr. Smith. You need a substitute. You need a defense attorney . . . an eternal advocate. And in Christ —and Christ alone—you've got one.

Extending Your Roots

Paul encouraged his readers to become reconciled to God. He also wants us to share his sense of responsibility for the redemption of others.

The idea of ministry is serving.

The idea of reconciliation is a change in relationship; being brought back together.

1. Read 2 Corinthians 5:11 to 6:2.

Fill in the blanks with words to help explain the meaning of ministry of reconciliation.

(1) Paul's steadfast purpose was to serve _ and the (vv. 13-14).

(2) He was controlled by the _____ .

(3) Two transformations occur for people who are "in Christ" (vv. 16-17).

(4) The miracle of "a new creation" is the work of God accomplished through _____ .

(5) We are Christ's _____ .

(6) As an ambassador for Christ, we should encourage others to _____ .

2. Write your own paraphrase of verse 21.

Growing Deep in the Christian Life: Salvation

1. The apostle Paul included your personal life in Romans 3. He continues to stress that all people stand guilty before God. Read the chapter from several translations. List the common excuses of people who refuse to admit they are sinners.

What are your excuses?

11 Three Crucial Questions

There are three crucial questions we must answer. Each has a two-word answer.

Question	Answer
1. Is there any hope for lost sinners?	Yes, Christ.
2. Isn't there any work for a seeker to do?	No, believe.
3. Is there any way for the saved to lose the gift?	No, never!

Now let me spell that out.

First question: Is there any hope for lost sinners? Yes, Christ. Not Christ and the church. Not Christ and good works. Not Christ and sincerity. Not Christ and giving up your sins. Not Christ and trying real hard. Not Christ and baptism, Christ and christening, Christ and morality, or Christ and a good family. No! Christ (period). Otherwise, it's works. He died for our sins and was placed in the grave as proof of His death. He rose from the dead bodily, miraculously, in proof of His life beyond. If you believe that He died and rose for you, you have eternal life. It's a gift.

Second question: Isn't there any work for a seeker to do? Don't I have to add to it? Answer: No (period). Believe!

One of my favorite illustrations of the importance of believing and not working is to consider a nice meal you and I enjoy together. You invite me over. I go to your home. We have planned this for quite some time, and you've worked hard in the kitchen. You have prepared my favorite meal. You are thrilled because you have a great recipe. And I'm happy because it's going to be a delightful evening with you. I knock on your door. I walk in and can smell the meal (ahh!)

all the way to the front door. I'm starved. We sit down to-gether at the table, and you serve this delicious meal. We dine and dialogue together. What a thoroughly enjoyable evening!

Then, as I get up to leave, I reach into my pocket and say, "Now, what do I owe you?" You're *shocked*! That's an insult. You knew what I needed, and out of love for me, you fixed it and served it. Why, a major part of being a good host is that you pick up the tab. For me to suggest that I'll pay for it is like a slap in the face. You don't even want me to help with the dishes. Love motivated your giving me this great meal. It is your gift to me. To ask to pay for it repels your love.

Do you realize that there are men and women all around the world who are reaching in their pockets this very day saying, "OK, God, how much do I owe You?"

I have communicated this same message for years, but I will never forget the time I had a lady come to the platform after a meeting to see me. She had dissolved in tears. She said, "Here's my Bible. Would you sign your autograph in the back, just your autograph? And then," she added, "would you put underneath it in quotes 'Salvation is a *gift*' "?

"You see," she explained, "my background is religious and all my life I've worked so hard. All my friends are from that same religion and they are all still working so hard. Now—for the first time in my life, I realize that God is really offering me a gift. The thing I have noticed about all of us, all these years, is that not one of us has ever been secure. We've never known that salvation was ours forever——because we worked so hard for it. Our plan was to keep working so we could keep it in us."

She had been reaching into her purse all these years, try-ing to pay God for His gift. Was it free? No, not really. It cost Christ His life at the cross many centuries ago.

Third question: Is there any way to lose the gift? No, nev-er! Now stop and think before you disagree. Stay with bibli-cal logic, not human reasoning. If you work for it, then you can certainly lose it. And that would mean it is not a gift; it's what you earned. We really confuse things when we try to turn a gift into a wage. Furthermore, just as no one can say how much work is enough to earn it, no one can ever say how little work is enough to lose it.

Salvation is simply a gift. It's simple, but it wasn't easy. It's free, but it wasn't cheap. It's yours, but it isn't automatic. You must receive it. When you do, it is yours forever.

1. Complete the Scripture search worksheet to find answers to three crucial questions.
(1) Is there any hope for sinners?

(2) Isn't there any work for seekers to do?

(3) Is there any way for the saved to lose the gift?

Locate Scripture verses or Bible people who support your answer to the questions. Write answers and summary statements in the appropriate areas.

Scripture Search Worksheet

Question	Reference
Hope for sinners?	
Work for seekers?	
Security for saved?	

1. Read book about eternal life or the security of the believer, making notes for future study.

12 | Two Possible Responses

We're back to basics, Mr. Smith. When you return to the roots of salvation, you can either believe and accept this gift, or you can refuse and reject it. And you can go right on living, by the way. You won't suddenly get struck by lightning if you reject Christ. I've noticed that God doesn't immediately start doing bad things to people who refuse His Son. He doesn't make you look foolish. He won't suddenly cut your legs off at the knees. He doesn't scar your face or make you lose your job. He doesn't keep your car from starting because you reject the message. He doesn't kill your closest friend or cause your mate to leave you as a judgment because you didn't believe. That's not the way God operates.

He simply waits.

And that fakes people out. That makes some folks think that if He really meant it, then He'd zap them for refusing to take His gift. No. Not necessarily. Those who think like that don't understand God. He holds out His grace and He makes it available even if we choose to reject it.

Extending Your Roots

Two choices are yours concerning salvation. You can believe and accept or you can refuse and reject God's gift.

1. Regardless of your choice, God's abundant grace is available. Read Romans 5:1-21. Look for the way the word *grace* is used. Perhaps you need to look up *grace* in a dictionary.

2. Meditate on verses 8, 15-17.
3. Write out Ephesians 2:8 in the space below.

Thank God for His gift.

1. A dialogue involves two people talking together about a certain subject. The setting for this dialogue was Jerusalem. The people involved are Jesus and Nicodemus.

Read John 3:1-21 and write the verses in dialogue style. Focus on Jesus' offer of a gift to Nicodemus.
NICODEMUS:
JESUS:
NICODEMUS:

2. More information about Nicodemus is found in John 7:50-52 and 19:39, 40. Add a concluding comment concerning the man's acceptance or rejection of the gift.

13 One Final Reminder

I must remind you of something: You don't have forever. With no intention of manipulating you, you need to remember that death is certain. I wish I had kept track of the funeral services I have conducted in the last ten years on behalf of those who died before the age of fifty. Without trying to sound dramatic, I think it would shock you to know how many die before they turn fifty. And I'm sure some of them thought, *I've got a long time to go.*

Listen, sin is terminal. And Mr. Smith, you've got that disease. It leads to death. It may not even be a year before you are gone and you will have thought you had plenty of time.

I'm sure Peter Marshall thought he had a long, long time. May I return to his life? He was appointed to the Senate chaplaincy in early January 1947, a specimen of good health. Yet it was a shade beyond two years that this forty-seven-year-old man was seized with a heart attack and died. He was as eloquent and creative as ever right up to the last-,but within a matter of hours, his voice was hushed forever. Only the printed page speaks for Marshall today.

A sermon of his that one can never forget is what he called "The Tap on the Shoulder."

> If you were walking down the street, and someone came up behind you and tapped you on the shoulder . . . what would you do? Naturally, you would turn around. Well, that is exactly what happens in the spiritual world. A man walks on through life—with the external call ringing in his ears, but with no response stirring in his heart, and then suddenly,

Growing Deep in the Christian Life: Salvation

without any warning, the Spirit taps him on the shoulder. The tap on the shoulder is the almighty power of God acting without help or hindrance . . . so as to produce a new creature, and to lead him into the particular work which God has for him.[1]

You may be feeling God's tap on your shoulder right now. If so, respond. Stop reading. Close the book, bow your head, and tell the Lord you have felt His tap—and you want to accept His gift of eternal life. Thank Him for giving you His Son, Jesus Christ.

If you have done that, Mr. Smith . . . you have just met your Substitute.

Extending Your Roots

Find a copy of Peter Marshall's sermons or prayers. Your public or church library may have his books. Or select a good biography about a modern-day Christian leader. Read his or her accomplishments for Christ.

1. Think about your accomplishments for Christ. What have you done recently for God?

2. List what you need/want to do for God while there is still time.

Taproot

1.   Write YES by the statements you truly believe or understand about the Substitute.

One Final Reminder

Jesus is God's Son.

Jesus was born of a virgin and lived a sinless life.

Jesus died on the cross for my sins.

Jesus is the only way to salvation.

Jesus was buried in a tomb and was resurrected on the third day.

Jesus is alive today.

Jesus is coming to earth again.

Jesus has prepared a place for me in heaven.

Jesus is my personal Savior and Substitute.

2. Locate a song, hymn, or poem about each statement. Learn the words and music. Perhaps you can make a personal hymnal about the Substitute. Gather the hymns to use in your daily worship time.

14 The Remedy for Our Disease

Something historic happened off the coast of South China, on a high hill overlooking the harbor of Macao.

Portuguese settlers, many centuries ago, spent ten years building a massive cathedral on that hill. It seemed imperishable to passersby. Many thought it would stand forever. But the awesome velocity of the winds from a typhoon literally reduced the thing to ruins. Everything except the front wall was leveled. The sheer wall, looking like one side of a massive fortress, stood alone against a deep blue sky. High on top of that wall stands a huge bronze cross, challenging the elements . . . almost as if to say to the winds: "You may tear down the other part of this cathedral, but you will not destroy My cross!"

In 1825 Sir John Bowring was in a terrible storm in that same harbor off the South China coast. Suffering shipwreck, he had no idea where to find land. Though it was in the light of day, the threatening skies and great swells blocked his ability to keep his bearings. If you've ever been in a storm at sea, you understand how easily one can lose perspective. Hanging onto the wreckage of his ship in the angry sea, sure to die, he caught sight of the bronze cross atop the old cathedral wall. The near-death rescue that followed was so dramatic, John Bowring was led to write several lines of poetry, expressing his gratitude to God for saving his life. Someone later put music to those words, and for over a hundred and fifty years God's people have sung Bowring's message, most of them knowing nothing of its origin:

In the cross of Christ I glory,
Tow'ring o'er the wrecks of time;
All the light of sacred story
Gathers round its head sublime.

When the sun of bliss is beaming
Light and love upon my way,
From the cross the radiance streaming
Adds more luster to the day.[1]

That which led to Bowring's rescue from the sea has led to our rescue from sin—the cross. But we need to understand that it isn't the cross itself that we honor. I know we refer to giving honor to the cross, and we are to lift up the message of the cross. But it isn't the literal cross we are to exalt. It isn't those original cross beams, those rugged, blood-soaked pieces of timber that stood on Golgotha centuries ago, that we honor. It is not the actual wood and nails. It is not its shape or it's location. It is the One who hung on it whom we honor. It is what the cross represents and the rescue it provides.

It was there our Substitute took our place. It was there the price for our sins was paid in full. It was the agony suffered on that cross that made the remedy for our disease effective.

No wonder so many of our Christian songs and hymns revolve around the subject of the cross. "Lift High the Cross," "At Calvary," "Am I a Soldier of the Cross?" "Down at the Cross Where My Savior Died," "The Old Rugged Cross," "When I Survey the Wondrous Cross," "Beneath the Cross of Jesus," "At the Cross," "Were You There When They Crucified My Lord?" "I Saw One Hanging on a Tree," and so many more, all familiar hymns the church has sung for centuries.

But again, remember the cross is merely the symbol of what we honor. You may remember that in the Old Testament era there was a time that God told the wilderness people of Israel to look upon a bronze serpent if they suffered from snakebite. He promised them relief if they would only look at that metallic snake that Moses had made and lifted up high on a standard for all to see. Those who refused to look died from the poisonous venom. Once the bronze carving served its purpose, once all those people were delivered from death, the Israelites were to discard the piece of bronze.

But if you ever make a study of that bronze serpent, you'd be surprised to discover that rather than discarding it, they dragged it around the wilderness and on into the days of the kings and the prophets. In fact, it became a fetish. They burned incense to it. Nothing wrong with the bronze serpent, and certainly nothing wrong with the idea, but it had served its purpose, and they wouldn't give it up. Finally, King Hezekiah was led of God to break it into pieces.

> He removed the high places and broke down the sacred pillars and cut down the Asherah. He also broke in pieces the bronze serpent that Moses had made, for until those days the sons of Israel burned incense to it; and it was named Nehushtan (2 Kings 18:4).

In the Hebrew tongue, *Nehushtan* means "a piece of brass." And that's all it was . . . nothing more than a piece of metal.

This may hit you pretty close to home, but the cross itself is a piece of wood . . . nothing more than that. Once it has served its purpose, the cross *itself* loses its significance. But the Savior who died on that cross lives on. And the redemption He provided continues to be significant and effective. He is our glory. He is the object of our adoration. So keep in mind, when we sing about the cross or when we speak of holding high the cross, that it is what that cross represents, the place where we gain our *spiritual* freedom. It was there our Substitute died in our place, providing the remedy for our spiritual disease.

The Remedy for Our Disease

 *Extending Your Roots*

1. Begin this study by reading the words of several hymns about the cross. Reflect on what the writer means by the word *cross*. Perhaps a book of hymn stories is available. Read the history of the hymn. What influence did the cross have on the writer? Select your favorite hymn about the cross and write the words below.

2. The bronze serpent was an Old Testament symbol that became more than just a symbol. Complete a study of this bronze snake. Begin with Numbers 21. Develop a series of questions using the suggested outline. Then provide the answers. Use a Bible dictionary as a resource.

WHO?

WHAT?

WHEN?

WHERE?

WHY?

3. Conclude with an explanation of John 3:14-15.

4. One final question:
HOW?

5. The Israelites could not accept the bronze snake as a symbol. They continued to drag the fetish with them through the years. Read about the final separation of the bronze serpent from the people (2 Kings 18).

Do you have a fetish you keep dragging around in your life? Something that is more than a symbol? Don't be a rabbit's-foot Christian.

 *Taproot*

1. The cross represents the place where we gain our spiritual freedom. At least three freedoms are the result of what our Substitute did for us on the cross.
(1) We are free to trust God to take care of our sins. Read Romans 6:15-23.
(2) We are free to live an abundant life. Read John 14:1-16 and John 8:30-32.
(3) We are free to live *in* Christ, *by* Christ, and *through* Christ. Search for Scriptures to support this freedom.

15 | A Prediction of the Substitute

Since we are living in a day when animal sacrifices are not performed, it's necessary that we familiarize ourselves with what that meant. Chances are good that most people have never even seen such a thing . . . though in biblical times such sacrifices were observed on a daily basis.

Even though the idea of offering up sacrifices seems strange to us, it was as common to people in the early days as the courtroom scene is to us today. You can hardly read a newspaper without reading of some courtroom scene. It's a daily affair—like "Perry Mason" reruns.

The sacrifices in ancient days were also daily affairs. Blood flowed freely out of places of worship. Deep-red blood-stains marked altars of stone and wood. For centuries sheep could be heard gagging and dying as priests slit their throats and poured the blood over an altar. You see, in those days they had priests in places of worship, just as we have attorneys in courtrooms today. In those days they followed the laws of Moses, just as we today obey the laws of the state and of our federal government.

But that which tied people together with the living God was blood sacrifice. Because it was so important, I want to familiarize you with some things that perhaps you haven't thought of before—and certainly things you've never seen before.

In the Old Testament there are two great predictions of Jesus' death on the cross—lengthy predictions. One is in Psalm 22 and the other in Isaiah 53. Psalm 22 emphasizes His person. Isaiah 53 emphasizes His work. Psalm 22 helps us hear the agony of Christ on the cross. Isaiah 53 causes us to appreciate the completed work of Christ which was predicted by the prophet. Isaiah's words describe our condition as well as the solution to our dilemma.

Our Condition

> Who has believed our message and to whom has the arm of the Lord been revealed? He grew up before him like a tender shoot, and like a root out of dry ground. He had no beauty or majesty to attract us to him, nothing in his appearance that we should desire him (Isa. 53:1-2, NIV).

What does all this mean? Among other things, there was nothing in Jesus' physique that was attractive. There was nothing in His person, as far as appearance was concerned, that caused Him to stand out from anyone else in His day. He looked like any other adult Jew. You would not have been attracted to Him had you lived in His day. There was no visible aura around Him or halo above Him. When He walked across the sandy path He got dirty like everyone else. When He slept He slept like everyone else. When He arose in the morning, I would imagine His hair was mussed just like everyone else's. He had all of the marks of humanity just like we have. The difference was that He was perfect within. In nature, He was not only man, He was God. But you couldn't tell it from the outside. That's what the prophet means when He says, "His appearance was not such that we would be attracted to Him." With the next stroke of his pen, Isaiah goes much deeper and addresses the sacrifice He paid.

> He was despised and forsaken of men, A man of sorrows, and acquainted with grief; And like one from whom men hide their face, He was despised, and we did not esteem Him (v. 3).

The Amplified Bible says, "We did not appreciate His worth."

There was no one in His day who realized the value of His person or the worth of His life. Oh, there were a few who believed and there were some who acknowledged that He certainly did the work of God. And there were some who believed He, in fact, was God. But most didn't have a true appreciation for Him that today, centuries later, many have. I've heard it said that in order for a person to be fully appreciated, to be seen as great, that individual needs to die and be removed from the earth for many, many years. Only then will some realize the person's greatness. So it is with many of our presidents and heroes, and so it is with Christ. Isaiah predicts, "We did not esteem Him."

The Solutions to Our Dilemma

So much for His person . . . now notice His work.

> Surely our griefs He Himself bore, And our sorrows He carried; Yet we ourselves esteemed Him stricken, Smitten of God, and afflicted (v. 4).

Notice, it was *our* griefs and it was *our* sorrows that He bore on *our* behalf. Not His. The burden of the cross was that He took the weight of that which was not His and carried it to the full. That explains our need for the Substitute. And people's response to Him? No respect! Our depravity blinds us. Therefore, we do not value His worth as the Bearer of our sins. Read on—

> But He was pierced through for our transgressions, He was crushed for our iniquities; The chastening for our well-being fell upon Him, And by His scourging we are healed (v. 5).

Peter picks up that same thought in his first letter:

> For you have been called for this purpose, since Christ also suffered for you, leaving you an example for you to follow in His steps, who committed no sin, nor was any deceit found in His mouth; and while being reviled, He did not revile in return; while suffering, He uttered no threats, but kept entrusting Himself to Him who judges righteously; and He Himself bore our sins in His body on the cross, that we might die to sin and live to righteousness; for by His wounds you were healed (1 Pet. 2:21-24).

Literally, the word "wounds" is singular. "For by His stripe, by His welt, His bruise. . . ." In other words, Peter pictures our Savior hanging on the cross as one massive welt, one awful bruise. He ought to know; he was there. The memory must have been a terrible one.

I will never forget an experience I had in elementary school when I was living in Houston. I was in the fifth grade at the time. Sitting in front of me was a classmate whose home life was nothing short of horrible. I'll never forget going to school one day and seeing maroon-colored stains on the back of his shirt as he sat in front of me. I called his name and said, "You have something on your shirt." He didn't want to talk to me about it. When we went outside for recess and I mentioned it again, he grabbed me and said, "Come here, I wanna show you something." So we went into the boys' room and he lifted his shirt. I had never seen such bruises and welts in my life. He told me he had been beaten by his father that morning. I found out later that his dad was an alcoholic. And it wasn't uncommon for the boy to be battered by his dad. My stomach turned as I looked across his back. I couldn't stand what I saw. It was like one massive bruise, so sore he could hardly bear anything to touch it. Just the slight weight of his shirt on his back was painful. Now when I read, "by His stripe (by His welt, by His bruise) we are healed," I always think of that boy's back.

But remember, this wasn't simply Jesus' back—this was His body. That's why Isaiah 53 describes Him as being pierced through, crushed, chastened, and scourged. Why? Why did that happen? The answer is in verse 6:

> All of us like sheep have gone astray, Each of us has turned to his own way; But the Lord has caused the iniquity of us all to fall on Him.

We need to be careful not to overdo the physical agony of the cross to the exclusion of the spiritual impact. Actually, the physical pain was not the worst part. It was the awful separation that occurred between the Son and the Father when "all our sin was laid on Him." For the first and only time, in all of time, the Father and the Son were separated, because God the Father could not look upon sin as all of it fell on Him. He turned away from His Son, causing the Lord Jesus to scream, "Eli, Eli, lama sabachthani . . . My God, My God, why hast Thou forsaken Me?" (Matt. 27:46). At that moment the Lord Jesus felt the crushing weight of all mankind's iniquity.

Extending Your Roots

When the word *blood* is mentioned in Christian conversations, most likely people are thinking about Jesus' sacrificial death or the sacrificial blood offerings of the Old Testament. These situations are certainly tied together.

1. Use the following guide to discover more about the Bible's use of *blood*.

(1) Pretend you are back in time. Moses is your spiritual leader. You and many people like you are seeking forgiveness for sin. Read Leviticus 1:1-5 and 4:1-7. Write out what your experience would include.

(2) Meditate on Hebrews 9:9-14.

(3) What does God really desire in sacrifice? (See 1 Sam. 15:22; Matt. 9:13; Mark 12:33.)

(4) Read Isaiah 53. How does Philip use this chapter to introduce the Ethiopian to the Substitute?

Growing Deep in the Christian Life: Salvation

The tabernacle has been completed. God is now ready to teach His people how to worship Him. Five key offerings were to be made by the Hebrews in order to have their sins forgiven and fellowship restored with God.

1. Beginning in Leviticus, chapter one, the five offerings are presented; each with specific instructions from God.

Complete the sacrificial offerings chart.

SACRIFICIAL OFFERINGS

Reference	Offering	Purpose	Fulfilled in Christ
Leviticus 1	(burnt)		
Leviticus 2	(grain)		
Leviticus 3	(peace)		
Leviticus 4	(sin)		
Leviticus 5	(guilt)		

2. What does it mean to say that Christ died for you?

16 An Explanation of the Sacrifice

Why was it necessary for Christ to die on the cross?

The explanation of His sacrificial death takes us back into the handbook of worship that the Jews used for centuries—the Book of Leviticus, chapter 4. From this chapter I want to show you four stages that occurred when someone came to offer a sacrifice before God. Once we see this, Christ's sacrifice will become much clearer.

In ancient days, when a sinner found himself or herself in sin, broken in fellowship with God, it was essential that there be an animal sacrifice. Sometimes the sacrifice was a goat, sometimes with a bull, sometimes with a heifer, or a sheep, or a dove, or even a pigeon. The details of such sacrifices are spelled out in this ancient book of worship used by the Jews and carried out by the priests—the Levites.

We find the process spelled out in four stages. *The first stage: The sinner brings an animal without defect to the altar.*

> Then the Lord spoke to Moses, saying, "Speak to the sons of Israel, saying, 'If a person sins unintentionally in any of the things which the Lord has commanded not to be done, and commits any of them, if the anointed priest who sins as as to bring guilt on the people, then let him offer to the Lord a bull without defect as a sin offering for the sin he has committed' " (vv. 1-3).

The plan was designed to be uncomplicated. As soon as one realized that sin had come into his life, intentional or unintentional, that individual knew that the sin had caused a separation from fellowship with God. To clear that up, an

117

animal had to be brought to an altar. Not any animal, but an animal that was without defect. The animal would become a "sin offering."

The second stage: The sinner lays his hand on the animal.

> And he shall bring the bull to the doorway of the tent of meeting before the Lord, and he shall lay his hand on the head of the bull (v. 4).

According to Leviticus 4, this is the job of the priest who, in this case, is the sinner. He lays his hand upon the head of the animal. Why did he do that? The act symbolized the transfer of guilt from himself to the animal. I cannot explain how such a transfer could occur, only that that was what God required. So the animal is brought and hands are laid on the animal.

The third stage: The animal is to be killed.

> But if he cannot afford a lamb, then he shall bring to the Lord his guilt offering for that in which he has sinned, two turtledoves or two young pigeons, one for a sin offering and the other for a burnt offering. And he shall bring them to the priest, who shall offer first that which is for the sin offering and shall nip its head at the front of its neck, but he shall not sever it. He shall also sprinkle some of the blood of the sin offering on the side of the altar, while the rest of the blood shall be drained out at the base of the altar: it is a sin offering 5:7-9).

Have you ever read anything like that before in your life? Just "nip" the neck so there is a sprinkling of the blood.

Every detail was so clearly defined. They were even instructed on *how* to offer the sacrifice.

Why the emphasis on blood, you wonder? Let me show you the key verse in the Book of Leviticus.

> For the life of the flesh is in the blood, and I have given it to you on the altar to make atonement for your souls; for it is the blood by reason of the life that makes atonement (17:11).

Look at the word "atonement." It's mentioned twice in this single verse. If you divide it into syllables, you come up with at-one-ment. God devised this plan: By the shedding of blood, two will be brought together as one. The blood of the animal will bring at-one-ment between humanity and God. The Hebrew term is *Chah-phar.* (Just think of the word *cover.*) The blood would cover sin.

This might be a good time for you to turn to the glossary of terms at the back of the book and check the words *atonement* and *redemption.* It was blood that bridged the gap.

Now back to Leviticus, chapter 4. We have seen the animal brought by the sinner. We have watched the hands of the priest being placed on the head of the animal. Next, the animal is slain at the altar.

The fourth stage: The blood is poured or sprinkled as God required.

> Then the anointed priest is to take some of the blood of the bull and bring it to the tent of meeting, and the priest shall dip his finger in the blood, and sprinkle some of the blood seven times before the Lord, in front of the veil of the sanctuary. The priest shall also put some of the blood on the horns of the altar of fragrant incense which is before the Lord, in the tent of meeting; and all the blood of the bull he shall pour out at the base of the altar of burnt offering which is at the doorway of the tent of meeting (vv. 5-7).

God required His priests to handle the blood ever so carefully— precisely according to His instructions. The details aren't important to us right now, but the significance of it is.

Since the earliest days, as these Jews connected at-one-ment with their Lord, there was a constant emphasis on blood and sacrifices. Sheep were slain at Passover by the thousands. The blood literally ran out of the city of Jerusalem. Priests were ceaselessly dealing with blood sacrifices. Day in and day out. *God required it.* That is why we must resist the modern tendency to remove the blood from our theology and our hymnody. Without blood, there is no remedy for sin.

But think of the treadmill of the ancient priestly task. Those of us who minister today know how, at times, some of our work can become a little monotonous. People on the outside usually don't think of it that way. But there are a few tiring and even repetitive assignments connected with the tasks of ministry. But nothing nearly *that* monotonous!

Just try to imagine killing the animals and pouring out the blood, killing more animals and pouring out more blood. Day after wearisome day . . . year after predictable year. Moffatt speaks of "the Levitical drudges"—because of the constant emphasis on the repetition of blood sacrifices.

But do you realize that these sacrifices never permanently took away sins? Never! The people found momentary relief from their guilt. They found temporary forgiveness. They went on their way rejoicing, which lasted for a while . . . but they'd soon be back with another animal.

And the focus? Sin. Sin. SIN! That's what caused Luther, when he finally turned the corner and realized the emptiness of his sin-repeating religion, to believe the good news concerning Christ. Prior to that it wasn't uncommon for the monk to be heard in his room repeating, "Oh, my sin, my sin, my sin, my sin, my sin." The weight of that sin filled his thoughts. There was an awful desperation in his prayers, though he did everything he could to make it work.

Do you have any idea how many religious people still live like that today? They have the same frame of reference. They live their lives with no more hope than those who brought animal after animal and pail of blood after pail of blood, altar sacrifice after altar sacrifice after altar sacrifice. And yet those Old Testament sacrifices never took away sins, not permanently . . . not until Christ.

When Christ died on that cross and once for all poured out His blood, He cried out, *"Tetelestai!"* "It is finished!"(John 19:30). The Greek term has as its root, *Telos*, "complete, end." "It's over. It's done. It's complete!" The sacrifice of the Lamb of God was once for all. We will never have to offer another sacrifice. It's not needed. His death on the cross finished the task.

Now that isn't my idea, it is what Hebrews, chapter 10, tells us.

> For the Law, since it has only a shadow of the good things to come and not the very form of things, can never by the same sacrifices year by year, which they offer continually, make perfect those who draw near. Otherwise, would they not have ceased to be offered, because the worshipers, having once been cleansed, would no longer have had consciousness of sins? (vv. 1-2).

Had the ancient priests' sacrifices been permanently effective, they would have walked away smiling, "Praise God. That's it. I'm through with all the animals, through with the altar, through with all the blood sacrifices." But that never could be said.

> But in those sacrifices there is a reminder of sins year by year. For it is impossible for the blood of bulls and goats to take away sins (vv. 3-4).

The writer continues the thought:

> By this will we have been sanctified through the offering of the body of Jesus Christ once for all. And every priest stands daily ministering and offering time after time the same sacrifices, which can never take away sins; but He, having offered one sacrifice for sins for all time, sat down at the right hand of God (vv. 10-12).

Christ never again has to die! After His one-time sacrificial death, the Father said, "I am satisfied." The cross payment satisfied the Father's demands against sin. How do we know He's satisfied? He raised His Son from the grave. He brought Him back from death. The resurrection was God's "Amen" to Christ's "It is finished." The theological word here is *propitiation*. (That's another good word to look up in the glossary.) What a mighty, liberating thought! The Father is completely satisfied. The cross absorbed all our sin and all the Father's wrath.

A practical message in all of this is that if God is satisfied with the death of His Son, and if I am in Christ, He is satisfied with me!

I don't have to live under the demanding enslavement of working, begging, pleading, fearing, bargaining, or paying penance to find favor with my God. In Christ, the Christian is as safe and secure as the Son before the Father. As one man once said:

Nearer, nearer,
Nearer, I cannot be,
For in the person of His Son,
I am as near as He.

Extending Your Roots

A little boy was told by his doctor that he could save his sister's life by giving her some blood. The six-year-old girl was near death—a victim of a disease from which the boy had made a marvelous recovery two years earlier. Her only chance for restoration was a blood transfusion from someone who had previously conquered the illness. Since the two children had the same rare blood type, the boy was the ideal donor.

"Johnny would you like to give your blood for Mary?" the doctor asked.

The boy hesitated. His lower lip started to tremble. Then he smiled, and said, "Sure, doctor, I'll give by blood for my sister."

Soon the two children were wheeled into the operating room—Mary, pale and thin; Johnny, robust and the picture of health. Neither spoke, but when their eyes met, Johnny grinned.

As his blood siphoned into Mary's veins, one could almost see new life come into her tired body. The ordeal was almost over when Johnny's brave little voice broke the silence. "Say, doctor, when do I die?"

It was only then that the doctor realized what the moment of hesitation, that trembling of the lip meant. Little Johnny actually thought that in giving his blood to his sister he was giving up his life! And in that brief moment he

had made his great decision! (Told by Myron L. Morris, in
Coronet, November 1948.)

1. In what sense is receiving Christ like a blood
transfusion?

 *Taproot*

1. The greatest day of the year for Israel was the Day of
Atonement. Read a description of this event in Leviticus
16:1-34. What is the distinction between sins covered and
sins completely cleansed and removed?

2. How does atonement apply to Christ? (See Lev. 17:11
and Rom. 3:25.)

3. Offer a prayer of thanksgiving to God for the perfect
sacrifice, Jesus Christ, and the fact that in Him the atonement is complete.

17 A Declaration of the Savior

The declaration of the Savior is found in the final verse of 2 Corinthians 5, which we looked at earlier in our study.

> He made Him who knew no sin to be sin on our behalf, that we might become the righteousness of God in Him (v. 21).

Remember the laying of hands on the animal? God the Father, as it were, placed His hands on His Son and said, "The sins of all mankind are transferred to You. At this moment You bear those sins." And He did. He did it on our behalf. That's the wonderful part of this message. He who knew no sin was made sin on our behalf. Christ, the spotless Lamb, took all our sin and guilt at the cross and cleared our debt. Why? "That we might become the righteousness of God in Him." I call that great news. Thankfully, it is all done. The work of salvation is finished work. It is provided for me as a sinner if I will simply come to Christ.

It is as if the Savior looks each one of us in the eyes and says, "I've paid your debt in full at the cross. If you come to Me, I will give you perfect righteousness."

My friend, Cliff Barrows, the song leader of the Billy Graham Crusade ministry, has ministered to many of us for years. We love him and his wife dearly. It is easy to forget that Cliff is also a husband and faithful father. Something once occurred in Cliff's home life that illustrates what I've been trying to say in this part of our study. Evangelist Billy Graham relates the story this way:

> My friend and associate, Cliff Barrows, told me this story about bearing punishment. He recalled the time when he

124

took the punishment for his children when they had disobeyed.

"They had done something I had forbidden them to do. I told them if they did the same thing again I would have to discipline them. When I returned from work and found that they hadn't minded me, the heart went out of me. I just couldn't discipline them."

Any loving father can understand Cliff's dilemma. Most of us have been in the same position. He continued with the story: "Bobby and Bettie Ruth were very small. I called them into my room, took off my belt and my shirt, and with a bare back, knelt down at the bed. I made them both strap me with the belt ten times each. You should have heard the crying! From them, I mean! They didn't want to do it. But I told them the penalty had to be paid and so through their sobs and tears they did what I told them."

Cliff smiled when he remembered the incident. "I must admit I wasn't much of a hero. It hurt. I haven't offered to do that again, but I never had to spank them again, either, because they got the point. We kissed each other when it was over and prayed together."

In that infinite way that staggers our hearts and minds, we know that Christ paid the penalty for our sins, past, present, and future.

That is why He died on the cross.[1]

And that is why, after his historic rescue off the South China coast, Sir John Bowring could write "In the Cross of Christ I Glory."

Extending Your Roots

Passover was the most memorable and oldest of Israel's sacrificial feasts. God instituted this event to celebrate Israel's deliverance from Egypt and what He had done for His children.

1. Read Exodus 12, noting how Christ as the spotless Lamb, stands out in this first passover. Make a list of your discoveries.

Growing Deep in the Christian Life: Salvation

2. Using a Bible dictionary or encyclopedia, learn more about each of the following topics.

The Paschal Lamb

Calvary's Lamb

Lamb of God

Worthy Is the Lamb

 *Taproot*

1. Picture again the suffering and death of Jesus, our SUBSTITUTE. Read aloud Luke 23:32-46. Also read the story about Cliff Barrows in this chapter.

2. Write a poem about this thought: Christ's sacrifice is now our Passover.

Notes

Part I

Chapter 1

1. I. G. Moss, "How Did the Universe Begin?" *Nature*, 8 August 1985, 316.

Chapter 4

1. J. Dwight Pentecost, *Things Which Become Sound Doctrine* (Grand Rapids, Mich.: Fleming H. Revell Co., 1955), 9-10.

Chapter 6

1. Mark Twain, *Familiar Quotations*, ed. John Bartlett (Boston: Little, Brown & Co., 1955), 679.
2. Michel de Montaigne, *Quote Unquote*, ed. Lloyd Cory (Wheaton, Ill.: Victor Books, 1977), 297.
3. Pentecost, *Things Which Become Sound Doctrine*, 17-18.

Chapter 7

1. John R. W. Stott, *Involvement*, Vol. I: *Being a Responsible Christian in a Non-Christian Society* (Old Tappan, N.J.: Fleming H. Revell Co., 1985), 64-65.

Chapter 8

1. Charlotte Elliott, "Just As I Am."
2. Catherine Marshall, *A Man Called Peter* (New York: McGraw-Hill, 1951), 319.

Part II

Chapter 9

1. Frank S. Mead, "Shepherd of the Senate," *Christian Herald*, November 1948.
2. Peter Marshall, "Mr. Jones, Meet the Master," *Mr. Jones, Meet the Master*, ed. Catherine Marshall (New York: Fleming H. Revell Co., 1950), 135-36.

Chapter 10

1. Charles Wesley, "And Can It Be That I Should Gain?"
2. Ibid.
3. Billy Graham, *How to Be Born Again* (Waco, Tex.: Word Books, 1977), 118-21.

Chapter 13

1. Peter Marshall, *Mr. Jones, Meet the Master*, 30-31.

Chapter 14

1. John Bowring, "In the Cross of Christ I Glory."

Chapter 17

1. Billy Graham, *How to Be Born Again* (Waco, Tex.: Word Books, 1977), 116.